Cambridge Papers in Sociology   No. 1

SIZE OF INDUSTRIAL ORGANIZATION
AND WORKER BEHAVIOUR

A

Cambridge Studies in Sociology

Size of Industrial Organization and Worker Behaviour

by GEOFFREY K. INGHAM

Lecturer in Sociology, University of Leicester

CAMBRIDGE
AT THE UNIVERSITY PRESS
1970

Published by the Syndics of the Cambridge University Press

Bentley House, P.O. Box 92, 200 Euston Road, London, N.W.1

American Branch: 32 East 57th Street, New York, N.Y. 10022

© Cambridge University Press 1970

I.S.B.N.s

0 521 07962 4 clothbound

0 521 09618 9 paperback

Library of Congress Catalogue Card Number: 78 120192

Printed by offset in Great Britain

by Alden & Mowbray Ltd. at the Alden Press, Oxford

Contents

List of Tables

Tables

List of Figures

Figure

Preface

This paper is a shortened and revised version of a dissertation approved by the University of Cambridge for the Ph.D. degree and is the result of research carried out during the years 1964-7.

Given the origins of this work a few remarks on its character and form are necessary. The work began as a critical examination of much of the research on what has become known as the 'size-effect' in industrial organizations. Briefly, this problem concerns the fact that there is considerable evidence to suggest that as the size of an organization increases member commitment or attachment (as measured by absenteeism, labour turnover, etc.) declines. These findings are discussed in detail in chapter 1. On the basis of this examination of the literature, a relatively small scale empirical investigation was carried out in order to further clarify some of the issues and evaluate, as far as possible, several hypotheses. I believe the research has led to the clarification of certain problems; but it would be too much to claim that many of the hypotheses have been subjected to any *critical* test. This is because a great deal of the theoretical understanding of the problems developed during the course of the empirical investigation; but unfortunately at a stage when it was impossible to allow these insights to guide the interviewing and other observations. However, I hope that many of the issues raised at an empirical level and in a more general abstract sense may have important implications for the sociological study of industry.

The writing of a piece of work such as this, which marks the beginning of a professional career, is only possible with the help and encouragement of one's teachers. In this respect I am very grateful to my research supervisor John H. Goldthorpe. I would also like to express gratitude to my former teacher and present colleague at the University of Leicester, Professor Ilya Neustadt. He originally stimulated and encouraged my interest in sociology.

In carrying out the field work for this research I was obviously dependent on the good will of many people. I am especially indebted to my subjects — those managers and workers in the Bradford engineering industry who allowed me to question them on their working lives.

Leicester   Geoffrey K. Ingham
December 1969

Part I

The Problem and Theoretical Considerations

1 The Problem

In this introductory chapter I propose first, to examine data which show the various behavioural and attitudinal consequences of organizational size[1] and second, to present the general problem with which this study will be concerned.

The general thesis concerning the 'size effect' is by no means a new one. In political science it has long been argued that democracy functions efficiently only in relatively small units.[2] Early sociologists were also familiar with the size problem. In his *Division of Labour in Society* Durkheim stated that:

> "...small scale industry where work is less divided displays a relative harmony between worker and employer. It is only in large scale industry that these relations are in a sickly state."[3]

Likewise, Marx[4] noted that the growth of large scale industry, by concentrating large numbers of men into organizations in which there was only minimal employer-employee interaction, was instrumental in arousing 'class consciousness' and in intensifying the conflict between capital and labour. In a different way Simmel[5] noted some of the structural changes that were induced by increases in size.

More recently, studies have been carried out by writers seeking to produce relatively precise evidence of this 'size effect' in industry by using various indicators of conflict and employees' attachment to their organizations. The main results in this respect have been as follows:

1 By *size* is meant the total number of employees within an organization.
2 For example, see: John Dewey, *Freedom and Culture* (New York, 1939), p. 159; Gunnar Myrdal, *An American Dilemma* (New York, 1944), pp. 716-19. For the classic analysis see Aristotle's *Politics*.
3 Emile Durkheim, *The Division of Labour in Society* (Glencoe, Ill., 1933), p. 356.
4 Karl Marx, 'Germany: Revolution and Counter Revolution', in V. Adoratsky (ed.), *Selected Works of Karl Marx*, vol. 2, p. 470 (New York, n.d.)
5 Georg Simmel, 'The Number of Members as Determining the Sociological Form of the Group', *American Journal of Sociology*, vol. 8 (1902).

Strikes

(i)   Cleland,[1] in his study of industrial organizations in the Trenton area of New Jersey has taken the incidence of strike activity to show a direct association between organizational size and management-worker conflict.

(ii) Revans[2] has used a similar index with data collected from the British nationalized coal industry and shows a direct relationship between colliery size and strike activity.

Absence

(i)   In the first of two research reports the Acton Society Trust[3] show that the correlation between size and the rate of absence for 18 collieries in the 'Pollockfield' area of the National Coal Board was $+0.667$ (sig. 2% level). Data from the Digest of the Ministry of Fuel and Power were recalculated by these researchers and showed a correlation of "more than $+0.60$" for absenteeism and colliery size throughout the industry as a whole. These findings were followed by an investigation into private industry of various kinds where the correlation between size and the rate of absenteeism proved to be $+0.447$ for 91 units (sig. level 1:500,000).

(ii) Revans[4] has noted that, in 67 gasworks administered by one of the regional gas boards, the correlation between absence and size was $+0.62$. Lateness may be classified as a form of absence and Revans similarly showed that there was a strong positive relationship between size of unit and the frequency of lateness per year in five randomly chosen gasworks.

(iii) In the second of two articles on the 'size effect' Indik[5] reports that, in a set of 32 delivery organizations, an index of 'member participation' derived from absence rates showed a significant negative correlation with size $(-0.53, p < 0.01)$.

(iv) Hewitt and Parfit,[6] in a study of a textile piece goods and hosiery

---

1   Sherril Cleland, *The Influence of Plant Size on Industrial Relations* (Princeton, 1955).
2   R. W. Revans, 'Industrial Morale and Size of Unit', *Political Quarterly*, vol. 27 (1956), and 'Human Relations, Management and Size', in E. M. Hugh-Jones (ed.), *Human Relations and Modern Management* (Amsterdam, 1958).
3   Acton Society Trust, *Size and Morale*, parts I and II (London, 1953 and 1957).
4   Revans, 'Human Relations, Management and Size'.
5   B. P. Indik, 'Organizational Size and Member Participation: Some Empirical Tests of Alternative Explanations', *Human Relations*, vol. 18 (1965).
6   D. Hewitt and J. Parfit, 'A Note on Working Morale and Size of Group', *Occupational Psychology*, vol. 27 (1953).

factory noted that their observed association between size and absence was statistically significant at the 5% level.

Accidents

(i)   The 'Pollockfield' data used by the Acton Society Trust[1] also showed a correlation of + 0.50 between the incidence of accidents and colliery size. The national figures also show that the rate of accidents per 100,000 man shifts worked increases with size of colliery.

(ii)   Revans[2] notes that there was a high and significant correlation (+ 0.96, sig. 3% level) between absence due to accidents and size of unit in five randomly chosen gas works.

Labour Turnover

(i)   Although he presents no data, Cleland concluded that labour turnover was generally lower in the smaller of his sample of over 80 plants.[3]

(ii)   Indik[4] shows that an index of 'member participation' derived from quit rates correlated negatively with organizational size ($- 0.34, p < 0.05$) in a set of 36 automobile dealerships.

Other Findings

Other studies have shown the relationship between size and miscellaneous attitudinal and behavioural patterns. The main findings are as follows:

(i)   Talacchi's[5] research revealed a correlation between size and a measure of general job satisfaction of $- 0.67$. A significant negative correlation was also found between the level of satisfaction and the level of absenteeism, but an examination of the labour turnover data and the level of satisfaction did not show any significant relationship, although a negative association had been hypothesized.

(ii)   Thomas[6] found that the quality of work performance and the 'degree of ethical commitment' were greater in the smaller of the welfare bureaux he studied.

(iii)   Campbell[7] discovered that as the size of the work group increased,

1   Acton Society Trust, *Size and Morale*, part I.
2   Revans, 'Human Relations, Management and Size'.
3   Cleland, *The Influence of Plant Size on Industrial Relations.*
4   Indik, 'Organizational Size and Member Participation'.
5   S. Talacchi, 'Organizational Size, Individual Attitudes and Behaviour: An Empirical Study', *Administrative Science Quarterly,* vol. 5 (1960).
6   E. J. Thomas, 'Role Conceptions and Organizational Size', *American Sociological Review,* vol. 24 (1959).
7   H. Campbell, 'Group Incentive Payment Schemes', *Occupational Psychology,* vol. 26 (1952).

the percentage of workers understanding the incentive payment scheme decreased and that this led to a reduction in the level of satisfaction with the system.

(iv) In discussing the mental health of the industrial worker, Kornhauser [1] concluded that large scale organization has a negative effect on mental health and, further, that this effect is to some degree independent of occupational differences.

(v) Marriott [2] found a low, but significant correlation between size of work group and individual output. However, in this connection it must be pointed out that Revans [3] has shown an association between output of coal per man year and size of colliery in which output increases with size to the middle ranges and then declines with increasing size.

The present study will be concerned solely with the relationship between industrial workers' rates of absenteeism and labour turnover and size of organization. The reasons for the exclusion of other phenomena such as strike activity and industrial accidents are, in the main, those of convenience. It was felt that to include these would have expanded the research to proportions which, within the limits set by time and resources, would have been unmanageable. Furthermore, the most recent work in this field (Talacchi and Indik), around which most critical discussion will take place, has concentrated on absenteeism and labour turnover.

For the research eight organizations, with certain common characteristics,[4] in the light engineering industry in Bradford were randomly selected from a list of firms compiled from the local trade telephone directory. The total sizes of the plants at the time absence and labour turnover data were collected[5] were as follows:

---

1   A. Kornhauser, *Mental Health of the Industrial Worker* (New York, 1965).
2   R. Marriott, 'Size of Working Group and Output', *Occupational Psychology,* vol. 23 (1949).
3   Revans, 'Industrial Relations, Management and Size'. The size-productivity relationship will be dealt with in more detail in the concluding chapter.
4   The type of technology, industry, skill level were controlled for various reasons which are discussed fully in this and subsequent chapters. A more detailed discussion of the sample of organizations is to be found in chapter 6.
5   The absenteeism and labour turnover data were collected between December 1965 and February 1966. The labour turnover figures are for the three years 1963-5. The absence data refer to the twelve-month period 1965 with the exception of two cases where the data were collected from the period December 1964 — November 1965. This was made necessary by incomplete absence records in the two firms.

A	5,000	(Departments x and y, 158)
B	3,000	(Department z, 90)
C	63	
D	26	
E	24	
F	16	
G	12	
H	9	

Plants A and B are branches of their respective enterprises, but all the small organizations are separate firms in their own right. The absence and labour turnover data were collected for semi-skilled and skilled workers only, and from the *whole firm* in the case of the small organizations. The figures for the semi-skilled and skilled men in plants A and B come from *departments* within the plants; two departments (x and y) containing, in all, 158 men were studied in plant A and in plant B one department of 90 workers was used.

Strictly speaking the absence and labour turnover data from the large plants should have been collected from each organization as a whole and not just from selected departments. Thus, it could be argued that my independent variable is department size rather than plant size. Two points are relevant to this problem. First, the reasons for this strategy were those of expediency. As we shall see later, it was necessary to control the possible effect of technology in analyzing the 'size-effect' and, therefore, only those departments with the appropriate technological system were considered. Also I wished to interview men from the organizations; but with limited time and resources I thought it better to have extensive coverage of one or two departments rather than draw a sample of about 60 respondents from a total population of over 8,000. Second, there are good reasons to believe that, in this case, it matters little whether the independent variable is size of plant or size of department. In the first place all three departments in the large plants were larger than any of the small firms. However, there is a more compelling reason to believe that this research design presents no serious problem. To anticipate the subsequent argument, it was decided that *bureaucratization* was the major structural variable linked to size and which was crucial in accounting for the behavioural patterns of the 'size-effect'. Consequently, it is only necessary to look at *bureaucratized sectors* of large plants in analyzing this particular problem.

Absenteeism

Measures of absenteeism, in investigations of this kind, are often expressed as days lost as a percentage of days scheduled to be worked per week or per year. However objections have been made to the use of this measure on the grounds that it includes cases of absence due to 'genuine' sickness which may often be quite lengthy and thus distort the absenteeism rate — especially in small organizations. It is argued that as absence is being used as an indicator of dissatisfaction or 'low morale', then rates compiled from short deliberate and 'uncertified' absences may be the best measure.[1] However, there are good reasons to believe that the *total* absence rate is equally suitable and that the distinction in question is not very meaningful. First, such a distinction neglects the fact of psychosomatic illness, which may be at least partly induced by a depriving work situation.[2] Similarly, it becomes difficult to deal with the size-accident relationship if short *deliberate* absences are viewed as the most important measure. Furthermore, I would like to suggest that the actual length of 'illness' may be, to some extent, deliberately calculated: that is to say, dissatisfied workers may be more reluctant to return to work after illness. Second, large bureaucratically controlled organizations are likely to be more stringent than the small firm concerning short 'uncertified' absences and consequently the worker in the small firm may have to convert his proposed two day absence into a week's 'certified' sickness. In this connection Trist and Hill[3] have shown that the frequency of sanctioned absences increases, whereas unsanctioned absences decrease with length of service. This is interpreted as showing a process of learning to substitute acceptable for unacceptable forms of absence. Thus, it is quite possible that some large organizations will have quite low levels of short deliberate absenteeism.

A way of getting round any problems set by very lengthy absences, and without using the dubious 'certified-uncertified' distinction, is to follow the procedure suggested by Turner and Lawrence among others. In their investigation they used a measure calculated from the number of *times*, not days, men had been absent from work in a one year period. Thus, a six-month absence and a one-day absence both count as *one* absence.[4]

Both the total time lost measure and the number of times absent measure have been used to deal with the data collected for the present research. However, before presenting the data we must note the reasons for calculating

---

1 See Acton Society Trust, *Size and Morale,* part I; A. Lundquist, 'Absenteeism and Job Turnover as a Consequence of Unfavourable Job Adjustment', *Acta Sociologica,* vol. 3 (1958).
2 Kornhauser, *Mental Health of the Industrial Worker.*
3 J. M. M. Hill and E. L. Trist, 'Changes in Accidents and Other Forms of Absence with Length of Service', *Human Relations,* vol. 8 (1955).
4 Arthur N. Turner and Paul R. Lawrence, *Industrial Jobs and the Worker* (Boston, 1965). However, this measure is also subject to certain weaknesses. Lengthy absences will reduce the opportunity for absence.

the absence rates for semi-skilled and skilled workers separately.[1] Several studies[2] have shown an *inverse* relationship between absenteeism and skill level and, therefore, the separate calculations have been made in order to eliminate any distortion in the comparison of organizations which may arise if the units in question differ in their relative proportions of skilled and semi-skilled men.

The relationship between organizational size and *total* absence is shown below in Table 1.1.

Table 1.1.   Total absence by size of organization and skill level

Size of organization		Total absence*	
		skilled	semi-skilled
A	5,000	3.98%	6.60%
B†	3,000	5.00%	7.62%
C	63	3.18%	1.15%
D	26	2.01%	1.60%
E	24	0.29%	3.00%
F	16	2.20%	0.39%
G	12	0.60%	0.85%
H	9	0.64%	0.70%

$$* \text{ Total absence } = \frac{\text{Total days lost per year}}{\text{Total days scheduled to be worked per year}} \times 100.$$

† This department comprised about 20% immigrants (mainly Pakistani). They were excluded in the calculation of the absence rates and from later interviews. However, this group showed strikingly similar rates of absence to the native workers.

For example, if a man is absent for three months only one absence is possible in that period. Therefore, the longer the periods of absence the less frequent will absence tend to be.

1 For the purposes of the present research men are classified as skilled only if they have served an apprenticeship. Unskilled workers, supervisors and apprentices were excluded from consideration.

2 For some of the many studies which show this relationship see: Gladys Palmer *et al.*, *The Reluctant Job Changer* (Philadelphia, 1962); Hilde Behrend, *Absence under Full Employment,* University of Birmingham Studies in Economics and Society, Monograph A.3, 1951; M. Baldamus, *Efficiency and Effort* (London, 1959).

The correlation between log size[1] and the total absenteeism rates proved to be highly significant for both skill levels, $r = +0.86$ (sig. 1% level) and $r = +0.94$ (sig. 1% level) for skilled and semi-skilled workers respectively.

The relationship between organizational size and average *number* of absences per man per year is shown in Table 1.2.

Table 1.2. Absences per man per year by size of organization and skill level

Size of organization		Absences per man*	
		skilled	semi-skilled
A	5,000	1.95	2.01
B	3,000	1.64	3.50
C	63	1.80	0.70
D	26	0.61	0.75
E	24	0.22	1.20
F	16	1.01	0.50
G	12	0.32	0.36
H	9	0.40	0.75

* Number of absences per man per year $\dfrac{\text{Total number of separate absences}}{\text{Total number of workers}}$

Again the correlations between log size and the absence measures proved to be highly significant. For skilled workers $r = +0.80$ (sig. 2% level) and for semi-skilled workers $r = +0.86$ (sig. 1% level).

Thus, there is a strong statistical relationship between the absence rate and organizational size in the sample in question here. In this respect the findings are consistent with those of the previously cited studies.

Labour Turnover

The findings of the previous research into the size-labour turnover relation-ship are, in fact, not consistent. The Acton Society Trust[2] found no signi-ficant correlation between voluntary turnover (quit rate) and size — although

1 Log size is used in all correlations. This procedure was followed by Revans and the Acton Society Trust where they also had a sample of organizations that differed widely in size.
2 Acton Society Trust, *Size and Morale*, part I.

a positive relationship had been expected. Similarly, the work done by Long [1] and the study carried out by the Institute of Personnel Management[2] also failed to find a significant relationship in this direction. On the other hand, Cleland[3] and Indik[4] do report such a relationship. To begin with two reasons may be suggested for this inconsistency. The first point concerns the adequacy of the way in which labour turnover has been measured. Usually, the quit rate is used; if, however, what is sought is an indicator of the level of organizational attachment among the majority of employees in the organization, then the 'stability rate' — that is, the proportion of long service workers in the organization — may be a more suitable measure. This measure would be especially useful in a situation in which an organization exhibited both a high quit rate and also possessed a large proportion of long service workers. For example, if a small number of unpopular jobs were causing a high quit rate it would be misleading to classify the total organization as comprising workers with a relatively low level of organizational attachment. Second, variables other than those usually considered by or of interest to sociologists are, of course, involved in determining labour turnover. For example, Long[5] and Cook[6] have demonstrated that there is a positive relationship between labour turnover and the level of employment; that is to say, in a situation of high unemployment there are fewer opportunities for job changing.

Therefore, *both* measures of labour turnover — the quit rate and the stability rate — have been used to interpret the data of the present study and the whole investigation was undertaken in the same city in order, among other things, to control the influence of the level of employment.

The average yearly quit rate for the years 1963-5 is shown in Table 1.3. The correlation between organizational size and the quit rate for the semi-skilled men proved to be of very low significance, $r = +0.69$ (sig. 10% level). For skilled men the relationship is even weaker, $r = +0.21$.

The stability rate which refers to the proportion of long service workers (over 10 years) in the organizations in question also failed to show any significant relationship with size, $r = -0.17$ (n.s.) and -0.12 for skilled and semi-skilled men respectively (Table 1.4).

---

1 J. R. Long, *Labour Turnover under Full Employment,* University of Birmingham Studies in Economics and Society, Monograph A.2 (1951).
2 Report of the British Institute of Personnel Management, Jan./June (1950); cited in Long, *Labour Turnover under Full Employment.*
3 Cleland, *The Influence of Plant Size on Industrial Relations.*
4 Indik, 'Organizational Size and Member Participation'.
5 Long, *Labour Turnover under Full Employment.*
6 P. H. Cook, 'Labour Turnover Research', *Journal of the Institute of Personnel Management,* vol. 33 (1961).

Table 1.3.   Mean Quit Rate by Size of Organization, and Skill Level

Size of organization		Mean quit rate* (1963-5)	
		skilled	semi-skilled
A	5,300	28.6%	38.1%
B	3,000	17.7%	35.2%
C	63	16.9%	44.9%
D	26	21.6%	20.0%
E	24	33.3%	16.6%
F	16	26.2%	16.6%
G	12	16.6%	0%
H	9	11.1%	16.6%

$$* \text{ Quit rate } = \frac{\text{Number of leavers per year}}{\text{Total number employed}} \times 100.$$

Table 1.4.   Stability Rate by Size of Organization and Skill Level

Size of organization		Stability rate* Over 10 years service	
		skilled	semi-skilled
A	5,000	45.0%	20.8%
B	3,000	38.5%	31.7%
C	63	30.5%	30.0%
D	26	37.5%	16.7%
E	24	16.7%	30.0%
F	16	16.7%	50.0%
G	12	100.0%	0%
H	9	66.6%	50.0%

$$* \text{ Stability rate } = \frac{\text{Number of long service workers}}{\text{Number of employees}} \times 100.$$

Thus, while we have seen that there is a strong statistical relationship between organizational size and the two measures of absenteeism, no significant relationship has been discerned between organizational size and various measures of labour turnover.

That the careful control of the labour market influences and the use of different labour turnover measures failed to produce a significant relationship between size and labour turnover suggests that the 'dissatisfaction/deprivation-withdrawal' model, from which the idea of a linear size-labour turnover relationship derives, is not an entirely adequate one for the present problem. Broadly speaking it is often implicitly assumed, in this type of approach, that industrial workers need to experience certain rewards of an expressive kind in the work situation. It is then demonstrated that these rewards are not present in certain kinds of organization – e.g. large scale – and this is often then put forward as the basis for a hypothesized size-labour turnover relationship. In a later chapter I will discuss critically the assumptions made in this type of approach and then suggest an alternative model which, it is hoped, will be able to deal with the problem in a more adequate way.

To summarize, then, there are *two* basic problems: first, to explain the observed relationship between organizational size and the level of absenteeism and second, to suggest explanations for the lack of a relationship between labour turnover and size of industrial organizations.[1]

---

1 The evidence concerning the size-absence and size-labour turnover relationships in this chapter should not be taken as tests of the *exact* nature of the relationship between these variables. Specifically, it is not possible to show the degree of linearity of the size-absence relationship due to the wide break in the sizes of the organizations – i.e. these range from 9 to 63 and then jump to 3,000. The major barrier to the collection of absence and labour turnover data from a large range of organizations whose sizes fell at frequent and regular intervals on a large/small scale was that of time. It was felt that the limited time available would be better spent on a detailed analysis of a few 'cases' – i.e. the organizations of this study. Moreover, I do not think that it is essential to my argument to show the exact nature of these relationships. All I am attempting to show is (i) that, consistent with the data of other studies, large plants have significantly higher rates of absence than small firms; and (ii) that in this study and several others there appears to be little difference between the labour turnover rates of large and small industrial organizations.

2 Size and Organizational Structure

In approaching the problem of the 'size effect' it is necessary to specify the intervening variables — that is, to identify those features of organizational structure that are associated with size and which are, in turn, likely to produce variations in rates of absenteeism and labour turnover. This has not always been attempted; the Acton Society Trust offer little in the way of explanation for their findings and Cleland does not go much further than singling out "the intangible personal approach" as the factor in his explanation of the 'size effect'. Talacchi and, especially, Indik have done the most rigorous work in this respect.

In his empirical study Talacchi[1] discusses the theory underlying his assumptions concerning the relationship between job satisfaction, absenteeism, labour turnover and organizational size, and postulates in this respect that the degree of functional specialization varies concomitantly with size. His main arguments are as follows. First, functional specialization narrows the work content and responsibility of the job, depriving it of non-material rewards such as pride in workmanship and recognition of achievement. Second, as regards interpersonal relations, increasing complexity of this kind together with the development of technical interests among departments and a reduction in their interaction, increases the potential for personal and group conflict. Both these factors are seen to lead to low levels of job satisfaction and high levels of absenteeism and labour turnover.

Indik's main formulations, though very similar to those presented by Talacchi, are more precise.[2] First, he hypothesises that an increase in size

---

1 Talacchi, 'Organizational Size, Individual Attitudes and Behaviour'. In passing it may be noted that although Talacchi makes these assumptions they remain at the above low level of specificity and are not used in the actual analysis. He works with the gross variables: size, the level of satisfaction, and absence and turnover. Thus, the important intervening variables are omitted.

2 Bernard P. Indik, 'Some Effects of Organizational Size on Member Attitudes and Behaviour', *Human Relations*, vol. 16 (1963). The only other relatively clearly defined set of hypotheses for the explanation of the 'size-effect' is that put forward by Revans ('Human Relations, Management and Size'). Revans states that 'administrative distance' between managers and men increases with size of organization and, therefore, that opportunities for mistakes and misinterpretations of reports develop — that is, management becomes less efficient. Second, Revans explicitly assumes that men expect their managers to perform efficiently;

increases the need for control and coordination which results in the growth of bureaucratization; impersonal modes of control are, however, ineffective in maintaining individual 'attraction' to the organization and, as a result, high levels of absence and labour turnover will occur. Second, Indik suggests that as size increases, so does the level of role specialization and that, as a consequence, the decrease in the degree of job complexity reduces the level of job satisfaction and tends to increase absence and turnover. Third, Indik suggests that there are potentially more communication linkages in large organizations than in small units and, therefore, adequate communication is less likely to be achieved. Less adequate communication reduces the level of interpersonal 'attraction' among members, and with this decline in 'attraction' absence and turnover are likely to increase.

Without examining these hypothesis in great detail it would seem that both Indik and Talacchi are asserting, first, (i) that large-scale organization reduces the *level of non-economic rewards* in the system, and (ii) that this type of reward is a *crucial* determinant of absenteeism and labour turnover. Second, Indik makes a rather different kind of statement in his first hypothesis when he suggests that a control system based upon impersonal rules is relatively ineffective in maintaining 'attraction' to the organization.

My first point by way of criticism concerns the fact that these two different kinds of statement have not, so far, been clearly distinguished from each other and that by doing this it may be possible to begin to deal with the problem of 'size-effect' more adequately. As most studies show that labour turnover varies independently of size it would appear that this phenomenon should not be dealt with as the same type of behaviour as absenteeism — that is, they should not be viewed as interchangeable and equally adequate indicators of, say, 'attraction' or satisfaction. The Acton Society Trust investigators came to similar conclusions in their first report.

> "There was, factory by factory, no significant correlation between voluntary turnover rate and total absenteeism, nor with size of factory.

and if they do not do so due to 'remoteness' from the work situation then 'morale' suffers (i.e. high absence, strikes and labour turnover). For several reasons I do not consider that this approach has any worthwhile contributions that could be incorporated into the explanation of this problem. First, he appears to assume that all industrial conflict can be reduced to 'bad communications' and that *all* workers are willing to cooperate with management and are merely frustrated in their aims by 'misunderstandings'. In this way he denies a 'real' conflict of interests between capital and labour. Second, he makes unwarranted assumptions about workers' orientations to work. Finally, it must be noted that Revans has no empirical data to support any of these assertions.

27

Hence it looks as if the reasons that cause men to leave their jobs are not those that cause them to stay away from them, whether for sickness or other reasons; but this conclusion needs to be investigated further." [1]

Quite simply, I would suggest that the problem of labour turnover can be best understood in terms of the relationship between the workers' levels and types of *expectation* from work and the structure of *potential rewards* in the organization; that is to say, the decision to leave or to stay in an organization will be dependent upon the level of rewards an individual receives in the system. On the other hand, absence behaviour can, I think, best be understood by referring, not only to the level of rewards, but also to the effectiveness of *inter*personal as opposed to *im*personal controls in determining the level of organizational *identification* [2] of those employees who have decided to *remain* in an organization. I hope the reasons for this strategy will become clearer as the argument develops. Therefore, in the next section which deals with the relationships between size and the intervening structural variables, the consequences of size for the structure of potential rewards and the level of organizational identification will be dealt with separately.

Basically, Indik and Talacchi point to the relationship, on the one hand, between size, functional *specialization* and *bureaucratization*; and, on the other hand, to the relationship between these latter two variables and job satisfaction, labour turnover and absenteeism. Such arguments are relatively well founded in the sociological study of work.[3] However, a number of qualifications are necessary with respect to the relationship between size and the two structural variables we have isolated.

FUNCTIONAL SPECIALIZATION

Two major points must be made with respect to this variable. First, the thesis of a direct relationship between size and organizational structure has recently

---

1 Acton Society Trust, *Size and Morale*, part II.
2 For the purposes of the present argument identification may be defined as the degree to which workers take the goals of the enterprise to be their own.
3 For some of the more thoughtful of the many studies see: Robert E. Blauner, 'Work Satisfaction and Industrial Trends in Modern Society', in Seymour M. Lipset and Walter Galenson (eds.), *Labour and Trade Unionism* (New York, 1960); *Alienation and Freedom* (Chicago, 1964) by the same author; C. Argyris, *Personality and Organization* (New York, 1957).

28

been challenged by Woodward[1] who has brought forward substantial evidence to indicate that, in manufacturing industry, task and organizational specialization is primarily a consequence of technology rather than of size, and furthermore, that there is no straightforward relationship between size and technology. Second, it will be argued that size has different consequences regarding specialization in the system of administration than it has in the system of production. Neither Indik nor Talacchi make it clear whether they are referring to the system of production and/or the system of administration. Moreover, it will be seen that if the behaviour of industrial workers is the focus of interest, then this distinction is of considerable importance.

The problem of specifying the exact nature of these relationships between size, technology and the level of specialization − in the system of administration and in the system of production respectively − can be made more manageable if these relationships are examined separately.

(i) Size and Specialization in the System of Administration

Recent evidence suggests[2] that, holding organizational goals and the imperatives of the technological system constant, size exerts a significant independent effect on the degree of specialization in the administrative system and especially in that part of the system dealing with 'human resources'. Simply, increases in size will mean that it becomes physically more difficult to deal with, for example, personnel problems and the control of workshop behaviour without an increase in the number of administrators and a subdivision of their tasks. If one assumes that an increase in the size of the labour force is accompanied also by an increase in production then similar exigencies will occur in that part of the administrative sector dealing with 'material resources'. In many small industrial organizations functional specialization does not extend beyond a small degree of delegated authority; the general manager − who is often also the owner − will act as buyer, sales manager, public relations officer etc. His immediate subordinate − works manager/ foreman − is likely also to act as personnel officer, inspector of products, and research and development officer etc.[3]

The fact that Woodward dismisses size as an important determinant of

---

1 Joan Woodward, *Management and Technology* (London, 1958); *Industrial Organization: Theory and Practice* (London, 1965).
2 C. R. Hinings *et. al.*, 'An Approach to the Study of Bureaucracy', *Sociology*, vol. 1 (1967); Richard F. Hall, J. B. Haas and N. J. Johnson, 'Organizational Size, Complexity, and Formalization', *American Sociological Review*, vol. 32 (1967).
3 For historical data on the process of managerial specialization see Rheinhard Bendix, *Work and Authority in Industry* (rev. ed.) (New York, 1963), pp. 211-15.

organizational structure would seem to stem partly from the exclusion from her sample of those firms employing less than 100 persons. The reasons for this strategy were that "the firms employing less than 100 people show no clear cut level of management between board and operators "[1] – that is to say, those firms in which size was of special importance were excluded from consideration.

(ii) Technology and Specialization in the System of Administration

The relationship between these two factors has recently been stressed in Woodward's work. Directly relevant to this discussion are the findings, first, that "the number of levels of authority in the management hierarchy increased with technical complexity" and second, that "specialization between functions of management was found more frequently in large batch and mass production than in unit or process production" – that is, the relationship between managerial specialization and technical complexity was curvilinear.[2]

(iii) Technology and Specialization in the System of Production

In this sector the level of task specialization is directly determined by the type of technological system. On the one hand, standardized product industries make possible the use of mass production technologies which seem to have gone furthest in the breaking down of tasks and work processes into minute subdivisions; whereas, in industries with less product standardization, the unit and small batch system retains a large variety in job content. Besides employing a more elaborate division of labour, technically complex production systems usually entail the creation of additional specialized jobs to deal with problems associated with the maintenance of the technical system itself.

(iv) Size and Specialization in the System of Production

There appears to be no evidence for a direct relationship between size and the level of task specialization in the production system. We shall see later that size, by influencing the level of bureaucratization of work procedure, may increase levels of specialization in the production system by, for example, reducing the levels of informal job rotation. However, the influence of these

---

1 Woodward, *Management and Technology*, p. 7.
2 *Ibid.* pp. 16-17. 'Technical complexity' means the "extent to which the production system is controllable and its results predictable" (p. 12). When production systems are classified in terms of this variable the degree of technical complexity increases from small batch and unit through large batch and mass to process production.

factors is relatively small and furthermore they can only work to produce variations within the limits set by the major determinant of task specialization: namely, technology.

In short, size and technology are both important in directly structuring the level of specialization in an organization's system of administration. In the case of the system of production, however, technology is almost exclusively involved in determining the level of task specialization, although size may exert a minor influence within the limits set by technology. These relationships are shown diagrammatically in Figure 1.

Figure 1. The Relationships between Size, Technology and Specialization

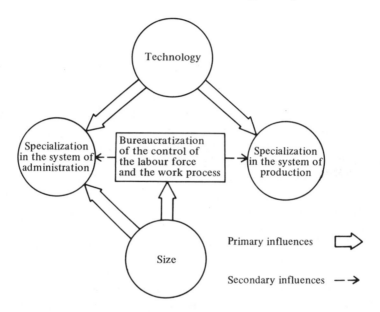

Thus, as there is little evidence to suggest that size and technology are directly related[1], then the type of technological system must be carefully controlled

---

1 Hinings, 'An Approach to the Study of Bureaucracy'; and Woodward, *Management and Technology*. There is, of course, a direct relationship between technological complexity and bureaucratization. That is to say, the more controllable is the technology and the more predictable its results the more readily can the whole working of the production system be subject to standardized and formalized procedural rules. However, as this relationship is not central to the present problem it has been omitted from the diagram.

in any study of the consequences of size for specialization in either the system of production or the system of administration, and also in the study of the consequences of these factors for worker behaviour.

We are now in a better position to examine the theoretical approaches of both Indik and Talacchi. First, Talacchi does not analyse the relationship between size and specialization nor the relationship between size and technology; thus, it is not clear whether his findings are 'size effects' or 'technology effects'. Furthermore, it is not clear whether he is dealing with specialization within the system of administration or the system of production, or both. Second, although Indik's theoretical paper[1] is open to the same criticisms, in his second paper which deals with an empirical investigation he selected organizations which were "highly uniform...with respect to technology, resources, growth potential and work methods".[2] In that part of Indik's empirical study dealing with size and specialization, the measure of job and task specialization was taken as the number of different job titles in the organizations. There are, however, reasons why this is not a suitable or reliable index for this particular problem; and this would seem to stem from a misunderstanding of the relationship between size and specialization in the different organizational sectors. It would follow from the discussion of the above four relationships that, holding technology constant, an observed relationship — based on Indik's measure — between size and the level of specialization in the total organization could, in fact, be caused almost solely by the level of specialization in the administrative system and need not say anything meaningful about the level of task specialization in the system of production. For example, factory X (2,000 employees) may have such formally defined job titles as welfare officer, sales manager, maintenance man, etc., whereas factory Y (100 employees) possesses few or none of these titles. In this case Indik's measure would show a far greater degree of job and task specialization in factory X. However, both factories may employ the same type of technology in which the majority of workers — that is, production workers — in both cases perform tasks which are more or less identical with respect to specialization. Thus, I would suggest that, in an analysis of size and specialization, the type of measure used by Indik is more useful in dealing with the administrative sector.

BUREAUCRATIZATION

Following Weber[3] many writers have pointed to and examined the relation-

1 Indik, 'Some Effects of Organization Size on Member Attitudes and Behaviour'.
2 Indik, 'Organization Size and Member Participation'.
3 Max Weber, *The Theory of Social and Economic Organization* (Glencoe,

ship between size and bureaucratization. It is, however, necessary to note that, although size affects the organizational structure of the administrative system with respect to such features as the number of hierarchical levels and degrees of specialization, etc., it is the consequences of the impersonal bureaucratic control of the system of production — that is, of the work process and the labour force — that has been, and is in the present case, the main focus of studies of the effects of size on worker behaviour. Thus, this particular problem requires that the impersonal bureaucratic mode of control is examined separately and not confused with other structural features of bureaucracy. To facilitate this distinction, these impersonal control mechanisms, characteristic of bureaucratic organization, will be referred to as consequences of *standardization* by which is meant the extent to which activities and roles are subject to procedural rules.[1] Thus, with this type of control system, authority relationships are essentially based upon norms of universalism, affective neutrality, and specificity.

A failure to examine carefully the relationship between the variables which form the constituent elements of bureaucracy — especially those connections between standardization and other elements — has led to difficulties in previous analyses of the relationship between size and bureaucratization. First, Terrien and Mills[2] have claimed that, because the task of control and coordination in an organization becomes more difficult as its size increases, then "...the larger the size of the containing organization the greater will

---

Ill., 1947), p. 338; see also John E. Tsouderous, 'Organizational Change in Terms of a Series of Selected Variables', *American Sociological Review*, vol. 20 (1955).

1 Hinings, 'An Approach to the Study of Bureaucracy'. *Standardization* is usually accompanied by written and filed communications, that is, by *formalization*. In their recent article Richard F. Hall *et al.* (Richard F. Hall, J. E. Haas and N. J. Johnson, 'Organizational Size, Complexity and Formalization', *American Sociological Review*, vol. 32 (1967)) conclude that *size* and *formalization* are only loosely related. However, it is significant that the relationship between size and what, from the point of view of the present study, I would take to be the most relevant aspects of formalization (authority relationships formalized in writing and the written stipulation of penalties for rule breaking), are relatively strong. The authors suggest that large scale organization does not necessarily lead to formalization as other control mechanisms such as *professionalization* may be present. (See Peter M. Blau, Wolf. V. Heyderbrand and R. H. Stauffer, 'The Structure of Small Bureaucracies'; *American Sociological Review*, vol. 31 (1966).) However, in the case of industrial organizations such mechanisms are unlikely to be present to any significant degree.

2 F. W. Terrien and D. L. Mills, 'The Effects of the Changing of Size on the Internal Structure of Organizations', *American Sociological Review*, vol. 20 (1955).

B

be the proportion given over to its administrative component". Evidence is produced which appears to support this hypothesis. Against this Anderson and Warkov[1] have argued, also on the basis of empirical research, that organizational size and size of administrative component are *not* positively related, and have in fact suggested the counter hypothesis that "the relative size of the administrative component decreases as the number of persons performing the same task increases". This latter assertion is consistent with the generalizations put forward by Woodward[2] and is the view held in this study. Despite this qualification, Indik has used the Terrien and Mills study as the basis for his assertions that size increases the need for control and coordination which, in turn, increases the number of individuals involved in this task which finally leads to bureaucratization and relatively ineffective impersonal mechanisms of control.[3]

Similarly, Bendix[4] does little to clarify the issue. Although he refers to bureaucratization in the sense of 'routine procedures'[5] Bendix considers that the most useful index of internal bureaucratization of economic enterprises is the proportion of administrative to production workers. Data from German industry led him to conclude that bureaucratization was highest in the smallest firms.[6] In other words, methods similar to those used by Terrien and Mills, and accepted by Indik, led Bendix to contrary and less plausible conclusions than those put forward by Indik.

There can be no doubt that large-scale organizations require impersonal mechanisms of control; in the absence of these procedural rules the alternative mode of control, in the case of industrial organization, requires a body of norms which are held in common by both workers and management. Caplow[7]has shown that interaction networks are patterned to some extent by the size of the group in as much as the number of potential relationships

---

1 T. R. Anderson and S. Warkov, 'Organizational Size and Functional Complexity; A Study in the Administration of Hospitals', *American Sociological Review,* vol. 27 (1961); Mason Haire, 'Biological Models and Empirical Histories of the Growth of Organizations', in Mason Haire (ed.), *Modern Organization Theory* (New York, 1959) also shows that the number of supervisors declines sharply with size.
2 Woodward, *Management and Technology.*
3 In a later study Indik shows that the span of supervisory control increases with size, but does not discuss the implications of this finding for his earlier theories. Bernard P. Indik, 'Relationship between Organization Size and Supervision Control', *Administrative Science Quarterly,* vol. 9 (1966).
4 Bendix, *Work and Authority in Industry,* pp. 211-26.
5 *Ibid.* p. 211.
6 *Ibid.* p. 222.
7 T. Caplow, 'Organizational Size', *Administrative Science Quarterly,* vol. 1 (1955); also *Principles of Organization* (New York, 1964), pp. 25-6.

increases at a faster rate than the number of members. Therefore, on the one hand, the more widespread level of interaction in small organizations may produce an interaction network with a high degree of 'connectedness',[1] and this will favour the development of norms which govern the instrumental activities within an organization.[2] For example, Gouldner's study[3] of the small gypsum plant shows that the 'indulgency pattern' was based on such norms, which were the produce of frequent and extensive management-worker contact. On the other hand, large organizations, that make it impossible for direct contact to occur between all members, inhibit such interaction and therefore favour the use of standardized and formalized procedural rules in the problem of the control of the labour force and the work process. Such rules are, in this case, important in the 'remote control' of the organization which, by virtue of its size, is difficult to deal with in

1 This concept is taken from Elizabeth Bott, *Family and Social Network* (London, 1957). Here it can be said to refer to the extent to which all possible combinations of interpersonal relations are realized within any one interaction network.

2 See Cleland, *The Influence of Plant Size on Industrial Relations;* Seymour M. Lipset *et al., Union Democracy* (Glencoe, Ill., 1956). This assertion is related to G. C. Homans' generalizations in *The Human Group* (London, 1950). Vertical interaction in industrial organizations is between persons of unequal status and this is the consideration which led Homans to modify his major generalization that '. . .the more frequently persons interact with one another the stronger their sentiments of friendship with one another are likely to be' (133). Thus, with the qualification, the statement becomes: "When two persons interact with one another the more frequently one of the two originates interaction for the other, the stronger will be the latter's sentiments of respect (or hostility) towards him and the more nearly will the frequency of interaction be kept to the amount characteristic of the external system." That is, the relationship is only likely to develop in the context that requires the interaction.
   The point is also similar to that made by Indik when he states that an increase in the 'average amount of communication' between members increases 'attraction' to the organization which, in turn, leads to lower levels of absenteeism and labour turnover. However, the formulation, as it is used in the present study, differs in three important ways. First, as Homans pointed out and as we shall see in more detail in a later chapter, an increase in the frequency of interaction does not necessarily lead to a greater degree of positive affect — there is a need to look at the *content* of the interaction. Second, not only is it the frequency of interaction, but also the degree of connectedness — on both the horizontal and vertical levels — that is important in making it possible for integration to be based upon interaction. Finally, Indik uses this formulation without noting its relationship with other variables — i.e. the level of bureaucratization — isolated for the explanation of the 'size effect'.

3 A. W. Gouldner, *Patterns of Industrial Bureaucracy* (London, 1955).

any other way;[1] that is, there is less chance that integration will be a product of interaction.[2]

Thus, in the main the difficulties in the studies mentioned above are not those of basic assumptions, but rather those concerned with the construction of a reliable index of the process whereby increases in size lead to organizational control on the basis of impersonal and standardized rules and procedures. That this enterprise has not been successful is apparent in the contradictory results of the work of Bendix, Terrien and Mills, and Anderson and Warkov. Furthermore, although the use of the administrative/production ratio index entails the assertion that impersonal modes of control vary concomitantly with the number of administrators in an organization (and this, in turn, with size) this has often been left implicit and little has been said about why this relationship should hold. It would indeed appear that there is little evidence for the assertion. Moreover, it could be argued that the opposite is the case: those organizations with a low proportion of administrators may, of necessity, use impersonal rules as an alternative to close and personal supervision.

In essence, the formulations of the present study differ from previous ones with respect to the analysis of the relationships between those elements of organizational structure responsible for the 'size effect'. We have seen that the analysis points to the fact that bureaucratization is most closely associated with size. Therefore, the next major task is to assess how bureaucratization affects, on the other hand, the structure of non-economic rewards and, on the other hand, the means of control and the level of identification in an organization.

Some Consequences of Variations in the Level of Bureaucratization for the Structure of Non-economic Rewards

The most important potential non-economic rewards in the industrial work situation can be divided into two main categories: activity or task rewards and social rewards. Social rewards can be further classified into those deriving from peer relationships and those stemming from interaction with superiors.

---

1 I do not wish to suggest that size is the only factor involved in the growth of a system of impersonal bureaucratic rules. The 'succession crisis' described by Gouldner points to another way in which this may occur.
2 The effects of technology are, of course, of great importance, in directing 'required' interaction. Nevertheless, the view is held that, holding technology constant, size will exert an independent effect on both 'required' and 'optional' interaction networks.

(i)   *The Structuring of Work Tasks*

Although technology, which has been shown to vary independently of size, is the main factor involved in the structuring of work tasks, the level of bureaucratization (standardization), in its association with size, may also exert influence in this direction. I am referring, here, to the standardization of work procedure which is a consequence of the necessity for control and coordination in a system where it is impossible for informal 'custom' to become the factory-wide basis for the organization of work.

Holding technology and skill level constant, one of the major consequences of the standardization of work procedures would seem to be in the area of 'job rotation'. Rigid and more or less permanent demarcation of individual 'spheres of competence' in the large plant simplify and thus facilitate control of the production process. It has even been suggested by Dreyfuss[1] that task specialization is a response to a management 'need', as it enhances their control over workers in as much as they become less dependent on the individual worker who can be more easily exchanged and replaced. However, in the small organization this is not quite the case; management is to begin with more dependent on the individual worker whose absence or withdrawal from the organization is more likely to disrupt the process of production than in the large firm. Thus, despite the fact that job rotation and diffusion of skills produces an even greater dependence on workers, these practices make for greater flexibility and stability in the small organization.

Flexibility in job demarcation is, of course, partly a consequence of weak union organization in small plants. In this case semi-skilled men may benefit especially as they are often able to perform tasks which, in most large unionized concerns, are reserved for men with an apprenticeship or similar qualification.

Thus, the less rigidly defined 'spheres of competence' in the small organization — made possible by the informal control of the work procedures[2] and the need for flexibility in the deployment of labour — may serve to increase the level of potential reward from the performance of the task.

---

1 Carl Dreyfuss, *Occupation and Ideology of Salaried Employees* (New York, 1938). Cited in A. W. Gouldner, 'Metaphysical Pathos and the Theory of Bureaucracy', *American Political Science Review,* vol. 49 (1955).

2 Gouldner, (*Patterns of Industrial Bureaucracy*) has noted this process with respect to the miners in the gypsum mine. "The informal work group and its norms, then constitute a functional equivalent for bureaucratic rules to the degree at least that it serves to allocate concrete work responsibilities and specify individual duties" (p. 164).

(ii) *Shop Floor Interaction*

Patterns of friendship at work are the possible result of many factors and there is no reason to believe that, under certain conditions, work groups cannot be as cohesive in large plants as in small ones. However, the level of standardization is likely to influence the nature of social relationships on the shop floor; for example, small organizations will tend to have less 'rationally' organized production methods which will allow for more frequent inter- action. I am thinking here not of the technological barriers to interaction[1] but of those barriers which are created by the formal and rigid control which is to be found in the large organization. For example, large firms often possess rules which prohibit workers leaving their job to talk informally and further constraints are imposed by the careful planning of production which leaves little time between the completion of one job and the start of another.

In some cases, the high level of 'connectedness' of the interaction net- works in the small plants may lead to the whole organization's becoming an informal 'work group'.

Thus, size is likely to be inversely related to the level of potential rewards from peer relationships.

(iii) *Authority Relationships*

Fewer levels of authority and frequent widespread vertical interaction in the small plant[2] will mean that impersonal 'bureaucratized' authority relation- ships will tend to be less predominant that in large-scale organizations. Thus, small plants are potentially the source of rewards stemming from the direct association with persons of superior status — i.e. managers and owners. Lockwood and C. Wright Mills[3] have both noted that association with superiors in small administrative units produces rewards in the form of 'status enhancement'; and an historical perspective reveals that prior to the growth of large-scale industry skilled manual workers gained satisfactions of a similar kind[4] Though this type of reward is unlikely to be acceptable to the

---

1 See Frank J. Jasinski, 'Technological Delimitation of Reciprocal Relationships', *Human Organization*, vol. 15 (1956); Charles Walker and Robert H. Guest, *Man on the Assembly Line* (Cambridge, Mass., 1955), pp. 66-80.
2 Juan Linz, *The Social Bases of West German Politics* (Unpublished Ph.D. thesis, Columbia University, 1959), cited in S. M. Lipset, 'Class Structure and Contemporary European Politics', *Daedalus*, vol. 93 (1964), p. 300.
3 David Lockwood, *The Blackcoated Worker* (London, 1958); C. Wright Mills, *White Collar* (New York, 1951).
4 See E. J. Hobsbawn, 'The Labour Aristocracy in 19th c. Britain', ch. 15, in *Labouring Men: Studies in the History of Labour* (London, 1964).

large majority of workers in contemporary Britain it may be a source of satisfaction in some cases — e.g. deferential workers. Conversely, a familiar complaint in the large plant — "I'm just a clock number" — concerns the lack of personal identity which is a consequence of impersonal methods of control. Thus, infrequent interaction may be a source of dissatisfaction in the large organization.

Bureaucratization and Identification

Small Firms

In small organizations the low membership allows for the large majority of potential social relationships to be realized. Consequently, the development of a system of norms which govern the instrumental activities of the organization may be reinforced by face-to-face interaction on both the horizontal and vertical levels. Thus, it is possible for workers to *identify* with the organization and its goals which, it may be added, are more 'visible' in small firms than in the large plant. This identification tends to engender commitment which, it is hypothesised, will reduce absenteeism.

Large Plants

I have argued that large scale limits the degree to which behaviour in the organization is governed by internalized norms and therefore impersonal bureaucratic rules comprise the basic control mechanisms. Goffman has suggested that "the loss of one's name can be a great curtailment of the self"[1] Although, of course, a close parallel cannot be drawn between the process of 'mortification of the self' in 'total' organizations and processes in large industrial plants, the use of numbers and not names and other depersonalizing factors are to be found throughout large organizations with high levels of bureaucratic control. Thus, identification will be minimized and, *ceteris paribus*, a sense of duty and obligation to the organization is unlikely to develop[2]

On the one hand, large-scale organization reduces the level of potential non-economic rewards in the system and it is often inferred on the basis of this evidence that labour turnover is likely to be at a higher level than in the small firm. On the other hand, the high level of dissatisfaction experienced by those who remain in a large plant in conjunction with the less effective

1 Irving Goffman, *Asylums* (New York, 1961), p. 18.
2 Cf. I. Smigel, 'Public Attitudes towards Stealing as related to the Size of the Victim Organization', *American Sociological Review*, vol. 21 (1956).

impersonal contacts may lead to higher levels of absenteeism than in a small firm where (*a*) dissatisfaction with the level of non-economic rewards is likely to be lower, and (*b*) where identification tends to lead to lower levels of absence.

3 Expectations from Work and the Role of Economic Factors

The foregoing discussion of the consequences of size for organizational structure and workers' attitudes and behaviour differs from previous work only in the details of the analysis of the structural variables. The assumptions concerning the reasons why these particular structural features should have this effect on worker behaviour are entirely consistent with those implied in the work of Talacchi and Indik. However, this procedure was followed merely for convenience: to enable a clearer analysis of the structural variables to be made. In this chapter I propose, first, to examine these assumptions and, second, to return to the statements of the first chapter and to suggest that the inadequacies of these assumptions account for at least some of the difficulties that have been encountered in the analysis of the size-labour turnover relationship.

The assumptions referred to above concern those aspects of work that industrial workers are supposed to value most highly or the 'needs' they must satisfy in order to maintain a level of satisfaction or reward sufficient to enable them to remain in their organization. However, it is difficult to specify the exact nature of the assumptions as they are never explicitly formulated. That these assumptions are necessary cannot be in doubt; the alternative is a form of 'behaviourism'. Basically, Indik and Talacchi imply that *all* industrial workers need to experience or, at least, value highly intrinsically rewarding work tasks and social relationships at work. Indik makes no distinction between peer and authority relationships and thus we must assume that he is suggesting that a degree of affect in authority relations is valued by workers.[1] The sources of these assumptions are not difficult to trace; in their eclecticism both Talacchi and Indik have incorporated theories and 'images' of industrial workers from *two* important traditions in industrial sociology.

In the first place, the assumptions concerning intrinsically rewarding work tasks stem mainly from work done in what might be called the 'alienation tradition'. Taking Marx's concept of 'alienation' various attempts have been made to use this to describe workers' feelings of deprivation especially in those organizations that utilize mass production techniques and, therefore,

---

1 Indik, 'Organization Size and Member Participation'.

offer only repetitive and fragmented work tasks.[1]

Second, Elton Mayo and writers in the broad 'Human Relations' tradition have concentrated almost exclusively on the way in which affective interpersonal relationships and work group cohesion determine workers' attitudes and behaviour. In his reaction to the individualistic bias in the theories of classical economics and early industrial psychology and from his conception of industrial society as being in a state of chronic and progressive anomie, Mayo was led to suggest that:

> "Man's desire to be continuously associated in work with his fellows is a strong if not the strongest human characteristic."[2]

In recent years it has been pointed out that 'Human Relations' writers have neglected the fact that the nature of interpersonal relations and the degree of work group cohesion are, to a large extent, governed by the technical structure of the organization. However, it must be noted that the writers who stress the role of technology have often incorporated typical Mayoite assumptions in their work. For example, Blauner states that:

> "For many workers the plant is a community, a center of belongingness and identification, which mitigates against feelings of isolation."[3]

Work which, broadly speaking, has developed from the original Mayoite approach, has suggested that expressive aspects of supervisory control are important determinants of industrial 'morale' and consequently of workers' attachment to and productivity in their organization. The implication here is that workers will value this type of authority relationship and automatically respond to controls which are accompanied by a degree of affect.

I would suggest that these types of theory, upon which Indik and Talacchi rely, first of all, tend to *over*emphasise the degree to which workers value or need to experience expressive aspects of work. Second, the failure to specify exactly the nature of these 'needs' leads one to assume, in turn, that these assumptions are 'universal' propositions or, at least, that variations in these

---

1 See G. Friedmann, *The Anatomy of Work* (London, 1961), pp. 139-45; Ely Chinoy, *Automobile Workers and the American Dream* (New York, 1955), pp. 85-6; and C. Wright Mills, *White Collar,* for the construction of an ideal type of 'craftsmanship' which is seen as the direct opposite of work in a mass production technology.

2 Elton Mayo, *The Social Problems of an Industrial Civilization* (London, 1949), p. 99.

3 Blauner, *Alienation and Freedom,* pp. 24-6, 113-15.

'needs' are of little importance in the analysis of industrial behaviour. Thus, with this type of approach workers' attitudes and behaviour are seen almost exclusively as responses to the impact of different work situations in which the crucial variables are work group cohesion and 'supervisory style', technological exigencies, or size and its influence on all these factors. Talacchi is quite explicit on this point:

> "Level of satisfaction or morale, as any motivational concept, is an 'intervening variable', which serves to mediate between *external stimuli* and behavioural *responses* on the part of individuals."[1] [Emphasis added.]

This overemphasis of workers' expressive 'needs' derives mainly from the 'Human Relations' critique of 'economic man' which, at one time, led to the concept's almost total and unwarranted dismissal.[2] As one of the leading writers in this school has said:

> "Elton Mayo destroyed the orthodox theory of worker motivation. For a time we tried to develop a theory of motivation that would leave out money altogether."[3]

Many studies of labour turnover seem to imply that workers will leave their employment if they fail to secure strong affective interpersonal relationships at work — but not, presumably, if their wage is too low.[4] It has been left to economists to continue to demonstrate the near truism that wage rates are often inversely related to levels of labour turnover.[5]

With respect to the overemphasis of the intrinsic rewards of the job itself

---

1 Talacchi, 'Organizational Size, Individual Attitudes and Member Behaviour', p. 400.
2 Mayo, *The Social Problems of an Industrial Civilisation,* especially ch. 2.
3 William Foote Whyte, 'Human Relations – A Progress Report', in Amitai Etzioni, *Complex Organizations: A Sociological Reader* (New York, 1961), p. 105.
4 In discussing, among other things, the role of financial incentives in worker motivation and labour turnover Mayo stated that: "The desire to stand well with one's fellows, the so-called human instinct of association, easily outweighs the merely individual interest and logical reasoning upon which so many spurious principles of management are based." *Social Problems of an Industrial Civilisation,* p. 39.
5 For example, W. A. Kerr, 'Labour Turnover and Its Correlates', *Journal of Applied Psychology,* vol. 31 (1949); B. L. Poidevin, 'A Study of Factors Affecting Labour Turnover', *Personnel Practice Bulletin,* vol. 1 (1949);

I do not wish to suggest that, for the majority of industrial workers, repetitive and fragmented work is not depriving. Rather, at a later stage, I will examine the possibility that the extent to which complex and demanding work is *valued highly* has been overemphasised for certain groups of workers. Moreover, my major criticism will be directed to the assumption that to leave the organization is a necessary behavioural response to dissatisfying work.

In the specific case of primary work group relationships, Mayo's diagnosis of industrial society's ills and his conclusion that solidary work groups may restore 'social health' has been at least partly responsible for the situation in sociology in which it is only quite recently that it has been suggested that the concept of the primary group, in its strict sense, is frequently inapplicable to industrial life. Dubin,[1] whose suggestion this is, notes that roles are inevitably segmented in complex industrial society and that although participation in one or more particular segments may be necessary it is not necessarily valued. Close primary relationships exist only in those situations where social experience is valued, and, as Dubin's data show, the industrial work situation is not defined as falling into this category by the majority of workers. Indeed, it may be added that active and extensive participation in work-centred relationships may clash with non-work commitments in the family and community etc.[2] – areas in which valued primary relationships are more commonly found.

In connection with the effectiveness of expressive aspects of authority relationships it must be stressed that the results of research along these lines have been notoriously inconsistent.[3] It would appear that, in the industrial situation, these factors cannot be held to be crucial determinants of workers' behaviour.[4]

In this brief analysis of the sources of some of the assumptions in work on

---

Long, *Labour Turnover under Full Employment.*
1 Robert Dubin, 'Industrial Workers' Worlds: A Study of the "Central Life Interests" of Industrial Workers', *Social Problems,* vol. 4 (1956).
2 For example, with respect to union participation and outplant commitments see: T. E. Kyllonen, 'Social Characteristics of Active Trade Unionists', *American Journal of Sociology,* vol. 56 (1951).
3 See H. L. Wilensky, 'Human Relations in the Workplace: An Appraisal of Some Recent Research', in C. Arensburg, *et al.* (eds.), *Research into Human Relations in Industry* (New York, 1957), pp. 25-50; and Michael Argyle, *et al.*, 'Supervisory Methods Related to Productivity, Absenteeism and Labour Turnover', *Human Relations,* vol. 11 (1958).
4 It has recently been stated that conflict and confusion result when attempts are made to combine expressive and instrumental elements in the foreman's role. Amitai Etzioni, *Complex Organizations* (Glencoe, Ill., 1961), pp. 118-25.

the 'size effect' three major criticisms have emerged. First, there has been a *neglect* of the part played by economic rewards from work. Second, there is the implicit assumption that the model of the industrial worker who is oriented to the attainment of a high level of non-economic rewards from work is the most useful and accurate. That is to say, there is little or no reference to *variation* in workers' 'wants'. Third, this general overemphasis on *non*-economic factors in 'sociologistic' studies has led to the neglect of the role of *remuneration* in the control of workers' behaviour.

Economic Rewards in Work

Although it ought not to be necessary to point this out, remuneration provides probably the most important source of reward (or deprivation) in industrial work. I do not wish to suggest that writers who have tended to emphasise non-economic rewards are not aware of this factor. This would be to overstate the case; rather, in their concern with the 'social' in economic life these writers are 'guilty' only by 'default'. Furthermore, I must stress that, although there is still a tendency in some branches of industrial sociology to direct attention to expressive features of work, my criticisms here are specific to work on the 'size effect'. Thus, we must add economic factors to our list of potential rewards in work. Figure 2 shows what can be considered to be the major rewards to be found in the industrial work situation.[1]

Figure 2.   A Classification of Potential Major Rewards
Received from Industrial Work

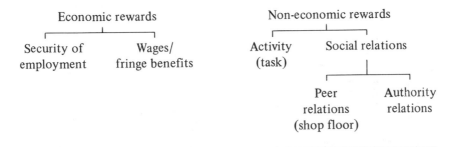

---

1   This classification of rewards is not meant to be completely exhaustive —
for example, the 'status' rewards of the skilled worker are not included.
However, I would claim that it includes the *major* rewards available to
industrial workers. Although, in some respects, this procedure is *a priori*
the classification does receive corroboration from Blauner's work ('Work
Satisfaction and Industrial Trends') of the main sources of satisfaction in

Variations in Wants and Expectations from Work

In the process of choosing employment the worker will be oriented to the attainment of one or more (or all) of these rewards from work. In other words, his 'wants and expectations' from work will be structured with these rewards in mind. In Indik's and Talacchi's formulation of the 'satisfaction equation' only two factors are to be found: namely, the structure of potential rewards and the level of satisfaction. The level and type of expectation without which statements about the level of experienced rewards or satisfaction cannot be adequately made is entirely neglected in their work. Sociology in general has long been concerned with the relationship between expectation and satisfaction, but in the somewhat parochial field of industrial sociology Morse's work on this relationship has to a large extent gone unheeded.[1] In a recent, and otherwise excellent, study[2] satisfaction is discussed entirely without reference to expectation.

Despite the criticism of the 'Human Relations' image of the industrial worker the present writer's intention is not to return to the concept of 'economic man' nor to follow Whyte's suggestion and construct a new model of 'socio-economic man',[3] but rather to allow for *variation* in workers' wants and expectations from work and to look upon these as possibly significant *independent* variables in explaining behaviour and attitudes in industrial organizations. The basis for this kind of approach is exemplified in Dalton's work on the 'industrial rate buster'.[4] In this analysis he shows that those workers who produced in excess of the work group production norms were from socially different backgrounds, and consequently *defined* work and the work situation in a different way, from those workers who complied with group norms and controlled output. More recently, Goldthorpe has extended this type of analysis in criticising the exponents of the 'socio-technical systems' approach for their implication that industrial behaviour is critically moulded by the roles of the socio-technical system. He argues

---

industrial work. Furthermore, the accuracy of the classification can be examined by looking at the workers' responses to the questions "What do you most like about working at your present firm?" and "Suppose you were looking for a job what would be your most important consideration?" (part II, chapters 8 and 9).

1 Nancy Morse, *Satisfaction in the White Collar Job* (Ann Arbor, 1953).
2 Blauner, 'Work Satisfaction and Industrial Trends'.
3 William Foote Whyte *et al., Money and Motivation* (New York, 1955). See especially pp. 1-8.
4 Melville Dalton, 'Worker Response and Social Background', *Journal of Political Economy*, vol. 55 (1947); 'The Industrial Rate Buster: A Characterization', *Applied Anthropology*, vol. 7 (1948).

that workers' wants and expectations relative to work — that is, their orientations to work — should be granted a certain degree of independence. With this approach it then becomes possible to deal with situations in which industrial behaviour and attitudes vary despite socio-technical similarities[1] Goldthorpe's explicit propositions are as follows:

(*a*) "That industrial workers do not enter different kinds of employment in quite a random manner in terms of their social characteristics, but rather tend to form labour forces which are in some respects 'self-selected' and thus in some respects relatively homogeneous.

(*b*) "That this homogeneity will frequently be greater than could be explained in terms of limiting factors such as ability, training, skill-levels, etc.; it will also result, and in particular under conditions of full employment, from workers making *choices* between different kinds of employment available to them, according to their existing wants and aspirations relative to work.

(*c*) "That in this way, members of labour forces of particular enterprises, or more probably sections of these, will tend as collectivities to have a distinctive orientation towards work and to inject a certain set of meanings into their work situation; these meanings will then play an important part in determining their behaviour within this situation.

(*d*) "That since the homogeneity in question results from individual choice of employment — that is, from a process of self-selection — the sources of the *specific content* of orientations to work and of definitions of work situations will to some significant extent be located externally to the industrial enterprise and pertain to non-work aspects of the individual's total life situation; for instance, to his community, to his status position and experience of social mobility, etc."[2]

It is interesting to note in this connection that a recent study by Turner and Lawrence,[3] which was based initially on the traditional lines of attempting to show workers' responses to variations in job complexity was, in fact, forced to look for other variables as no significant relationship was found for the

---

1 John H. Goldthorpe, 'Attitudes and Behaviour of Car Assembly Workers: A Deviant Case and a Theoretical Critique', *British Journal of Sociology,* vol. 17 (1966).
2 John H. Goldthorpe, 'Orientation to Work and Industrial Behaviour: A Contribution to an Action Approach in Industrial Sociology', Unpublished paper (Cambridge, 1964).
3 Turner and Lawrence, *Industrial Jobs and The Worker.*

sample as a whole between an index of job complexity and an index of job satisfaction. It was discovered that sub-populations of workers brought different 'predispositions' to work and thus responded *differently* to very *similar* work tasks. For example, certain large groups of workers with a low level of expectation responded with a relatively high level of satisfaction to jobs which were low on task complexity, whereas other groups of workers were dissatisfied with the same level of complexity.

At this stage of the argument it must be made clear that *orientation* is not synonymous with 'need'; nor are orientations necessarily based on workers' 'needs' in the psychological sense. This distinction can be illustrated by a brief examination of Argyris' work.[1] By concentrating on the psychological level of analysis Argyris makes explicit assumptions about workers' 'needs' and according to this theory there is a basic incongruence between the 'needs of the mature personality' and the requirements of formal organization. In the transition from infancy to adulthood, personality is seen to develop from a state of passivity to a state of activity, from dependence to independence, etc. Argyris then demonstrates that the requirements of formal and technical organization demand that workers are passive, dependent, etc. From this standpoint he suggests that a high emphasis on 'money and other material rewards' is an individual adaptation to a work situation which creates psychological conflict and frustration. However, I would suggest that, as an additional interpretation, a desire for material possessions is a *culturally prescribed goal* which, under certain conditions, will outweigh any need for 'self-actualization'. I am not suggesting that theories of the kind put forward by Argyris are totally inapplicable to the analysis of industrial behaviour, but rather hope to show that without allowing for, and specifying *exactly*, the variations in culturally based orientations to work, these theories are often inadequate. Once again it is possible to illustrate from Argyris' work. He suggests that there are several modes of adaptation to frustrating work situations; these are 'defence mechanisms' such as 'daydreaming' or quitting the organization.[2] However, without an analysis of the worker's definition of the work situation — that is, ultimately of his wants and expectations from work — then the important prediction concerning which alternative will be taken cannot be made.

Basically, it is useful to classify workers' wants and expectations — that is,

1 Chris Argyris, *Personality and Organization* (New York, 1957); 'Understanding Human Behaviour in Organizations: One Viewpoint', in Mason Haire (ed.), *Modern Organization Theory* (New York, 1959), pp. 115-54; 'The Organization: What Makes it Healthy?', *Harvard Business Review*, vol. 36 (1958).
2 This, in itself, is an advance on the simplest 'dissatisfaction-withdrawal' model.

orientations — in terms of the importance attached by the worker to economic and non-economic rewards of various kinds in considerations about job choice. This procedure yields four 'basic' orientations. Of course, the classification may be as elaborate or as simple as the problems under investigation demand. Using the classification of potential rewards in Figure 2 a very complex typology of orientations could be constructed; but, I believe the simple classification presented below is adequate for the present analysis.

(*i*)   High economic; high non-economic requirements from work.
(*ii*) High economic; low non-economic requirements from work.
(*iii*) Low economic; low non-economic requirements from work.
(*iv*) Low economic; high non-economic requirements from work.

Although wants and expectations from work, in so far as these are involved in job choice, are to be viewed as independent variables it would be a mistake to see these existing independently of the types of employment available to workers in any situation under consideration. In other words, orientations must always be viewed in terms of the structure of 'ends' from the actor's point of view.

In the present case the organizations in question are likely to differ in the degree to which they are potential sources of non-economic rewards. Also, like Cleland[1], it was found that the small firms paid much lower wages[2] than the large plants. Thus, we have a situation in which *the small firms offer a high level of non-economic rewards and a relatively low level of earnings: whereas, the large plants offer lower levels of non-economic rewards and high wages.*

On the basis of these arguments it can be hypothesised that:

(*i*)   workers who are oriented to the maximization of their earnings and who place low emphasis on non-economic rewards [(*ii*) above] will tend to seek, in this situation, large high-wage plants for employment. Furthermore, if workers whose wants comprise both high earnings and a high level of non-economic rewards [(*i*) above] are unable to find an organization to meet these requirements they will tend to give priority to economic wants and choose large high-wage plants.

Therefore, in both these cases, and especially in the first, there will exist a relatively high degree of *congruence* between expectations from work and the level and type of reward. Thus, labour turnover will be low and this is most likely to take the form of a high stability rate.

1 Cleland, *The Influence of Plant Size.*
2 The wages paid in the small firms were between £3 and £6 per week lower than in the large plants. See part II, chapter 7.

The organizations studied by Goldthorpe and Argyris seem to provide examples of this type of high congruence. Both these plants possessed all the features which have usually been assumed to lead to high levels of labour turnover — that is, they were large scale plants employing predominantly semi-skilled workers. Despite these factors, in the study reported by Argyris,[1] management considered the plant to be one of their best as, among other things, labour turnover was at a low level. Other evidence from this study suggests that satisfaction with the high level of remuneration was a factor involved in this behaviour. And, similarly, Goldthorpe found that *despite* feelings of deprivation and dissatisfaction labour turnover was at a *low* level[2] due to the workers' satisfaction with the high wages. Such workers may be said to be *economistic* in their orientation to work; that is, they are concerned with securing high wages often at the expense of non-economic rewards. Thus, in the pursuit of high wages, the activity of work and the contingent social relationships are often invested with *instrumental* rather than *expressive* significance. Therefore, this particular syndrome of wants and expectations from work may be termed *economistic-instrumental.* The use of *both* the French (*l'economisme*)[3] and English (*instrumentalism*)[4] terms is not arbitrary. This rather clumsy terminology has been used because it is possible for economism — that is a sensitivity to wage issues and the pursuit of high earnings — and instrumentalism to vary independently. For example, workers of the kind referred to by type (iii) above are *non*-economistic and instrumental. Such workers view work solely as a means to an end in so far as they do not pursue non-economic rewards in work; but neither do they seek high wages. In other words instrumentalism may be used to describe the definition of work as a 'means to an end' but it does not necessarily imply anything about what these 'ends' are.

Similarly, we can hypothesise that:

(ii) workers whose wants and expectations comprise relatively low remuneration and high non-economic rewards [(iv) above] will tend to choose small, low-wage organizations with a low level of bureaucratization.

Therefore, in this case also there will exist a high level of *congruence* between expectation and reward. Thus, the stability rate in such organizations will be relatively high. This orientation to work may be termed *non-economistic-expressive* in so far as non-economic rewards are defined as worth pursuing as ends in themselves. The argument thus far is summarised below in

---

1 Argyris, 'The Organization: What makes it healthy?'.
2 Goldthorpe, 'Attitudes and Behaviour of Car Assembly Workers'.
3 A. Touraine and O. Ragazzi, *Ouvriers d'Origine Agricole* (Paris, 1961).
4 Goldthorpe, 'Attitudes and Behaviour of Car Assembly Workers'.

Table 3.2 which shows labour turnover as a function of (*a*) orientation to work, and (*b*) the level and type of reward in the organization.

Table 3.2.   Labour Turnover by Orientation to Work and Size of Organization

	(*a*) Orientation to work	
	Economistic-instrumental	Non-economistic-expressive
Large scale:	*High* congruence[1]	*Low* congruence[2]
Low non-economic rewards	*High* stability rate/*Low* quit rate	*Low* stability rate/*High* quit rate
High remuneration		
Small scale:	*Low* congruence[3]	*High* congruence[4]
High non-economic rewards	*Low* stability rate/*High* quit rate	*High* stability rate/*Low* quit rate
Low remuneration		

(*b*) Level and type of reward

Cells 1 and 4 represent the strain towards congruence, between orientation to work and the structure of rewards, in a situation of *full employment* – i.e. extensive job opportunities. Thus, the labour turnover estimates for these organizations are those which are likely to occur in this 'ideal-typical' situation. In the case of the large-scale organizations employing pre-dominantly workers with an economistic-instrumental orientation, stability rates will be relatively high due to the motivation to maximize earnings in the long run. I do not wish to suggest that standardized and fragmented work tasks performed in an impersonal atmosphere can become sources of a high level of reward, but rather that, on the one hand, certain groups of workers

51

place relatively low emphasis on rewarding work and a very high emphasis on economic rewards. Thus, the absence of complex work tasks and solidary work groups is not experienced as especially depriving. Again, some other groups of workers may, in fact, experience psychological deprivation in the work situation of a large organization; however, the stability rate will not necessarily be low because of the subordination of these feelings of deprivation to the goal of the long run maximization of earnings. Thus, I am arguing that *it is a mistake to infer the automatic behavioural response of quitting the organization from the observation of feelings of dissatisfaction or deprivation.* Empirically, it may be the case that large scale organizations will often employ workers with orientations other than economistic-instrumental, and conversely small scale organizations may employ workers with such an orientation, for a short period. However, the low level of congruence between expectation and reward in these cases will mean that *very high* quit rates will tend to occur among these workers (cells 2 and 3). If we assume a high level of employment and an availability of ends (i.e. suitable firms) from the actor's point of view, such incongruent relationships may be viewed as errors in self-selection due to faulty information or complete ignorance of the situation. Several studies have shown that in a cohort of workers who join an organization those who are likely to leave do so after a short period of time (within six months), whilst the remainder are likely to stay and become long service workers.[1] These findings suggest that many workers' orientations are incongruent with the available rewards and almost immediate withdrawal results. Thus, as we are looking at the act of quitting the organization as a result of two factors — orientation and reward — this adds weight to the contention that large and small organizations need not differ in their quit rates. There is no reason to believe that workers in small firms make fewer 'errors' in self-selection than those choosing large plants.

In conclusion it must be stressed that the basis for *all* orientations to work is an instrumental one. If, in a situation of full employment, the level of earnings in a given plant fails to rise above a certain level, high rates of labour turnover will occur whatever the orientation to work.

Remuneration as a Means of Control

Earlier it was pointed out that analyses of the 'size effect' have stressed the fact that large-scale organization leads to impersonal methods of control and thus inhibits workers' identification with the organization which, in turn, leads to high levels of absenteeism. However, such formulations which are

---

1 For example, E. L. Trist and J. M. M. Hill, 'The Representation of Labour Turnover as a Social Process', *Human Relations,* vol. 3 (1953).

concerned with what may be termed the *normative integration* of industrial enterprises are based on the implicit assumption that values and norms held in common by both management and workers are the most important source of integration. This concern with 'social cohesion' is once again a legacy of Mayo's interpretation of industrial society. However, this approach diverts attention from the fact that the integration of the industrial enterprise is primarily based not upon shared norms and values but upon economic exchange – the 'cash nexus'. Etzioni has recently pointed out that, in comparison with other types of organization, the *involvement* of lower participants in economic organizations is *calculative* rather than moral in character and, therefore, that the power exercised by management is *remunerative* rather than identive[1]. To suggest, as Indik does, that impersonal controls are ineffective and viewed with 'repugnance' by members does not allow the focus of attention to fall on the main means of control in industrial organizations. With Etzioni's classification in mind it is clear that large scale plants are near to the ideal type of Utilitarian organization[2] – that is, controls exercised by management are almost exclusively remunerative. However, I would suggest that, in small firms of the type I have described, workers are to some extent *morally* involved in the enterprise in so far as their involvement is based, at least in part, on identification. That is to say, these workers are not merely attached to their organization by the cash nexus – but are, in effect, committed. Thus, a degree of *identive* power (the power derived from the ability to make people identify) may be exercised by management in small firms[3].

---

1   Etzioni (*A Comparative Analysis of Complex Organizations*) suggests that *involvement* refers to the orientation of the subordinated actor to the means by which he is controlled. This is determined by the degree to which the superior's power is considered legitimate and by the degree to which the superior's actions are congruent with the action the subordinate would desire. Three major types of involvement are presented:
(i) *Alienative* involvement designates an intense (high affect) negative orientation.
(ii) *Calculative* involvement may be positive or negative, but is characteristically an orientation of low intensity (affect).
(iii) *Moral* involvement is a positive orientation of high intensity (affect).
Moral involvement is often referred to as *commitment* and in a recent article, 'Organizational Control Structure', in James March (ed.), *Organizations* (Chicago, 1965), pp. 650-77, Etzioni suggests that *identification* is a major characteristic of such involvement.
2   Etzioni, *Complex Organizations.*
3   The distinction between 'rewards' and 'control structure' is in some instances only an analytical one. For example, for the instrumentally

A word here is necessary about the acceptance of such controls by the workers. Identive power cannot replace remunerative control; the former is only likely to develop in a situation where (*a*) the basic economic 'wants' of the workers are met, and (*b*) when such modes of control are found to be *acceptable* by the lower participants. The acceptance or rejection of identive means of control is not solely dependent upon the structure of authority relationships in the enterprise. High levels of management-worker interaction may not lead to organizational identification *per se*. In this respect it may be hypothesised that workers in the small firms who are responsive to a degree of identive power tend to *evaluate* management-worker relationships as those of co-operation and consensus. Moreover, this definition of the situation is to be seen as existing in some degree independently of such intra-organizational features as frequency of interaction. For example, the highly co-operative 'gaffer and man' relationship that Stacey found in the traditional industries of Banbury was not solely a result of the internal structure of the firms in those industries. The acceptance of management's leadership in the small traditional firm was inextricably linked with the stable and accepted status distinctions of the community's total system of stratification:

> "In the traditional sector economic, social, religious and political values and attitudes are closely linked and traditional industry closely related to the total social system."[1]

Control Structures, Involvement and Absence

Large Plants

It has been assumed in many studies that in large plants high levels of dis-satisfaction, from various sources, lead to high levels of absenteeism as a response to this 'role strain'. Further, impersonal controls are seen to be ineffective in generating identification and therefore there are, from the

---

oriented workers a high level of economic rewards means not only low labour turnover, but also responsiveness to the remunerative controls. Similarly, the worker who values association with superiors as an important reward will therefore respond to identive controls.

1 Margaret Stacey, *Tradition and Change: A Study of Banbury* (London, 1960). Of course, other types of community will produce different evaluations of authority relationships. For example, it has been noted that working class communities that are characterised by close knit kinship and friendship networks and little inter-class interaction can lead to the evaluation of authority relationships as those of conflict and antagonism. See David Lockwood, 'Sources of Variation in Working Class Images of Society', *Sociological Review*, n.s. vol. 14 (1966).

worker's point of view, few 'moral' barriers to absence. However, I do not consider this type of approach to be entirely convincing or meaningful. We have just seen that Utilitarian organizations are not dependent on workers' commitment, but rather that they rely on calculative involvement. Thus, in the large plant, *all* barriers to absence are not removed merely by the workers' lack of identification. In this situation, the workers' behaviour will be influenced by the nature of his calculative involvement. Absence from a dissatisfying work situation may be desirable, from the worker's point of view, but of course this would also involve a loss of earnings. Thus, the levels of absence in the large plant will be, to a large extent, determined not only by the levels of dissatisfaction and identification, but also by the level of the workers' economic wants. Very high absence is probably a consequence of dissatisfaction and deprivation in the work situation, a low level of organizational identification *and* a relatively low level of expectation with respect to earnings. However, even a highly instrumental orientation of the type described in the last section is unlikely to be associated with very low levels of absenteeism. Three or four absences per man per year may result in only a slight reduction in earnings but form a relatively high absence rate.

Small Firms

In the small firms of the type I have described low levels of absence have been assumed to be due to low levels of dissatisfaction and a degree of 'moral' involvement on the part of the labour force. Here, a further word is necessary on the type of influence job satisfaction is likely to have on absence behaviour. The type of assumption usually made is that (*a*) satisfying work (activity and social relationships) 'attracts' workers to the organization and tends to reduce absenteeism, and (*b*) that dissatisfying work 'repels' workers and increases absenteeism. However, these two assumptions are not necessarily linked and, further, I would suggest that (*a*) is not entirely true. A worker may enjoy the rewards of complex and demanding work and satisfying social relationships at work, but the fact that he is involved in this activity for about 200 days of the year will tend to diminish its 'marginal utility' *vis-a-vis* a day off work. However interesting the industrial worker's activity may be, only in certain rare instances is it likely to cause him to reduce absence due to sickness – that is, to go to work unfit. In other words, there is likely to be a direct relationship between deprivation and absence, but not an inverse relationship between non-economic reward and absence. Very low absence rates (below 2%) such as those we have seen for the small firms of this study are probably the result not only of low levels of dissatisfaction, but also of the workers' *moral involvement*. To the employee who is involved in such a way work is defined as more than labour (however interesting) for economic reward; it may be seen as a duty and moral obligation.[1]

Thus, we may hypothesize that:

Rates of absenteeism vary inversely with the level of moral involvement of the labour force.

However, the other main point of the above discussion has been to suggest that the level of moral involvement (identification) is not the only factor involved in the explanation of variations in rates of absenteeism. I have suggested that, in an organization where moral involvement is almost entirely absent, there is also likely to be an *inverse* relationship between the level of the workers' economic wants and the rate of absenteeism.

---

1 This analysis differs from my earlier formulations, 'Organizational Size, Orientation to Work, and Industrial Behaviour', *Sociology*, vol. 1 (1967), in several ways. First, a clearer distinction has been made between *rewards* and type of *involvement*. In this article the concept of involvement was used in an unclear way: task rewards were included as a determinant of involvement which in essence should refer *only* to the *evaluation* of social relationships in the organization — and especially authority relationships. Although there is an obvious relationship between rewards and involvement in certain instances (see note 3 p. 53) I have decided to make this distinction which is, therefore, part analytical and part empirical. Consequently, the level of congruence between expectation and rewards is related to the labour turnover problem only. Absenteeism is dealt with by referring to different types of control structure and involvement. Furthermore, a simpler classification of orientations to work is used in the present study.

4 The Independence of Orientations to Work

It is essential to the approach of this study that the independence of orientations to work is demonstrated: otherwise, it could be assumed that *all* variations in orientation are the result of a process of socialization within the *immediate* socio-technical system or that industrial behaviour is best understood merely as a response to the exigencies of this formal organization.

The discovery by Goldthorpe[1] of attitudes and behaviour which differed, in certain respects, from that usually associated with assembly line plants adds weight to the contention that orientations to work must be viewed, to some degree, as independent variables. However, in the case of the present problem, where the socio-technical systems differ in their levels of bureaucratization, two other methods may be used in an attempt to test this proposition.

First, certain methodological strategies may be used: for example, careful and direct questioning of respondents regarding their requirements in work would be a straightforward and useful method of establishing the independence of their orientations.[2]

Second, it is desirable that an attempt should be made to trace and specify the *sources* of differences in orientation to factors external to the employing organization. We have noticed that an important difference between large- and small-scale firms, at least in certain industries, is the discrepancy between the average rate of earnings they provide and that workers are likely to differ in the degree to which they act towards the maximization of their earnings. Weber,[3] among others, has noted the relationship between work and norms governing types and levels of consumption and saving. The phenomenon of the 'backward sloping supply curve' of labour[4] was used to illustrate the 'traditional' as opposed to the economically 'rational' orientation to work.

1 Goldthorpe, 'Attitudes and Behaviour of Car Assembly Workers'.
2 Ideally a study of the orientations of the workers who have left an organization in order to compare them with those of the workers who remain should have been carried out to deal with this problem. However, for several reasons this was not altogether possible in this research. First, some of the firms were not willing or able to provide names and addresses of leavers and second, the main body of interviewing left little time for either interviewing or sending postal questionnaires.
3 Max Weber, *The Protestant Ethic and the Spirit of Capitalism* (London, 1930).
4 This was used to illustrate the way in which the amount of labour brought forth begins to fall off once a critical level of pay has been reached.

Therefore, an examination of certain styles of life within the working class with a special focus on the reference groups and normative constraints which regulate the motivation to maximize earnings may provide important clues to the problem of 'self-selection' to small, low-wage organizations and large, high-wage organizations.[1] That is to say, the problem is basically one of attempting to account for variations in the degree to which workers are oriented to the maximization of their earnings.

At most I feel able to put forward only tentative suggestions in this respect. Consequently, part II, chapter 10, which deals with the relevant empirical findings can, at best, only be looked on as exploratory.

In attempting to trace the sources of a highly economistic-instrumental orientation to work one must look to those factors which may lead to a weakening of 'traditional' working class styles of life. Basically, the 'ideal type' construction of the 'traditional' working class[2] points to the way in which the highly connected and cohesive kin networks and relatively stable and undifferentiated working class communities lead to the placing of definite limits on the level and type of consumer behaviour.

The process of the breaking down of these norms or the isolation from them by certain groups of workers has been clarified theoretically in recent years[3] and the most important point for our present purposes is that made by Lockwood[4] when he suggests that the 'privatization' of the worker by isolating him from traditional working class norms may lead to his taking the mass media as his point of reference in his consumer behaviour and thus cause a greater preoccupation with the maximization of earnings.[5]

---

1 For example, R. D. Shepherd and J. Walker, 'Absence from Work in Relation to Wage Level and Family Responsibilities', *British Journal of Industrial Medicine,* vol. 15 (1958), show a curvi-linear relationship between absenteeism and family size; the fact that high levels of absence are associated with large family size suggests that 'styles of life' and not merely economic exigencies are involved in determining absenteeism.
2 See David Lockwood, 'The New Working Class', *European Journal of Sociology,* vol. 1 (1960); David Lockwood and John H. Goldthorpe, 'The Manual Worker: Affluence, Aspirations and Assimilation', Unpublished paper presented at the Annual Conference of the British Sociological Association, Brighton, 1962; Josephine Klein, *Samples from English Cultures,* vol. 1 (London, 1965), especially pp. 121-215.
3 David Lockwood and John H. Goldthorpe, 'Affluence and the British Class Structure', *Sociological Review,* n.s. vol. 11 (1963).
4 Lockwood, 'The New Working Class'.
5 This hypothesis is consistent with work done by Katz and Lazarsfeld in which they show the function of 'primary' groups in mediating between the direct influence of the mass media and consumer behaviour. See E. Katz and P. Lazarsfeld, *Personal Influence* (Glencoe, Ill., 1954).

At this stage I think it is useful to distinguish between changes in working class styles of life brought about, on the one hand, by geographical mobility, rehousing and the subsequent weakening of kin networks and, on the other hand, those changes which may be the result of social mobility influences. First, 'privatization' brought about by geographical mobility and rehousing in new towns or estates may have the effect of making these workers more 'consumption-minded', but this is not necessarily a change to a middle-class style of life.[1] Second, social mobility, in various ways, may effect life styles within the working class. For example, the son of a 'white-collar' worker in a manual occupation may, in fact, retain some aspects of middle-class standards which require a preoccupation with securing high earnings.[2] In a similar way, intra-generational mobility may also lead to middle-class influences. Studies have shown that many industrial workers − especially semi-skilled workers who are not committed to any one particular occupation − have had widespread experience of non-manual work of various kinds.[3] There may also be a group of 'aspiring' workers who are subjected to middle-class influences, regardless of their own mobility experiences, through the status superiority of their wives or siblings. In addition to these direct middle-class influences the 'privatization-consumption-mindedness' hypothesis will also apply to these workers as their aspirations will mean that they are integrated to only a low level with either the working or middle-class and, therefore, are unlikely to be part of a highly connected kin network which could set strict limits to the level and patterns of their consumption.

Apart from class and status factors, life-cycle differences may also be of considerable importance in this respect. For example, young, newly married men may be constrained to secure high earnings through sheer economic exigency.[4]

The first step in accounting for a non-economistic-expressive orientation is to show the absence of those factors which may lead to a preoccupation with securing high earnings. However, the absence of this pressure does not explain why non-economic rewards are valued and why close interpersonal authority

1 Lockwood and Goldthorpe, 'Affluence and the British Class Structure'.
2 On some of the consequences of downward mobility in this respect see: H. L. Wilensky and H. Edwards, 'The Skidder: Ideological Adjustments of Downwardly Mobile Workers', *American Sociological Review,* vol. 24 (1969).
3 See, for example, Goldthorpe, *op. cit.,* 1964: S. M. Lipset and R. Bendix, *Social Mobility in Industrial Society* (London, 1959), pp. 169-71.
4 For discussion of attitudes to overtime and life cycles variables see Ferdinand Zweig, *The Worker in the Affluent Society* (London, 1961); S. Shimmin. 'Extra-Mural Factors Influencing Behaviour at Work', *Occupational Psychology*, vol. 36 (1962).

relationships can become a source of identification with the enterprise. On the one hand, *prior* job socialization is likely to be important in the development of expectations for complex and varied work tasks and social rewards. Also, it must be stressed that some socialization in the immediate work situation will occur among some workers. By suggesting that orientations can be viewed as *independent* variables, relative to the work situation, I do not wish to posit a set of fixed and immutable 'definitions of the work situation'. However, the emphasis of this study will be on *prior* orientations to work and not on any changes in orientation that might occur. On the other hand, the definition of the work situation as one of co-operation and consensus and the workers' identification with management's goals will almost certainly be found predominantly in rural or small town industry in which traditional inter-class relationships are observed in both workplace and community relations.[1] However, it is unlikely that structural factors such as these will be able to account for differences in orientation to be found in a single, large and occupationally differentiated urban area such as the one used in this study.

1 See Stacey, *Tradition and Change.*

5 Summary

The problem was defined initially as one of attempting to explain (*a*) the direct relationship between organizational size and rates of absenteeism, and (*b*) why no such relationship has been consistently found between labour turnover and size, though for various reasons this has often been expected.

The major structural features likely to be associated with size and also with variations in absenteeism and labour turnover were isolated: namely, the levels of *functional specialization* and *bureaucratization.* An examination of the relationship between size and these two structural variables led to the conclusion that, in the case of the industrial production worker, technology is a major determinant of functional (task) specialization and, further, that technology is not directly related to size. Thus, it was suggested that the type of technology and, therefore, the major variations in the level of specialization in the system of production were to be carefully controlled in any empirical investigation into the problem. The level of *bureaucratization* was shown to directly affect (*a*) the structuring of the level of non-economic rewards in an enterprise, and (*b*) the nature of the organizational control system. The conclusions in this respect were as follows:

(i)   The level of bureaucratization is directly related to task specialization (within the limits set by technology) which is, in turn, *inversely* related to the level of potential rewards from the activity or the work task.

(ii)   That size and the level of bureaucratization are *inversely* related to the degree of 'connectedness' of the interaction networks and the frequency of shop-floor interaction. Thus, there is an *inverse* relationship between size and the level of potential rewards from peer relationships.

(iii)   Bureaucratization is inversely related to the level of management-worker interaction in an organization. Therefore, in large plants impersonality may be a potential source of deprivation; whereas, small firms provide potential rewards for workers in the form of direct association with persons of higher status.

Thus, on this basis size was hypothesized to be inversely related to the level of potential rewards from non-economic sources which, in turn, was assumed, *ceteris paribus*, to be directly related to levels of labour turnover and absenteeism.

Bureaucratization is directly related to the level of impersonal controls in the organization. Impersonal controls were assumed to inhibit *identification* with the enterprise which was hypothesized to be *inversely* related to the level of absenteeism in an organization. In other words, it was suggested that impersonal controls were less effective than those based upon the employee's identification with the enterprise.

This type of approach, which is basically similar to that of previous studies, was criticized for neglecting the role of *economic rewards* in assessing satisfaction and for making certain assumptions about workers' 'needs'. The main criticisms in this respect were directed to the fact that these assumptions were left implicit — that is, *expectation* from work was not analysed sufficiently well. This type of approach was further criticized for omitting to mention the role of *remuneration* as a means of control in economic organizations.

It was then suggested that an explicit formulation of the possible *varieties* of workers' wants and expectations from work — that is, of their orientations to work — would be useful in explaining those cases in which there was a lack of association between size and labour turnover. Specifically, it was hypothesized that workers tend to *select* for employment those organizations which are likely to be commensurate with their wants and expectations from work. In short, the relatively low quit rates and high stability rates in large, high-wage plants suggested that they tended to attract workers with a highly *economistic instrumental orientation*. Thus, it was asserted that the high levels of economic rewards would tend to reduce labour turnover despite any dissatisfaction with the level of non-economic rewards that might occur in such plants. On the other hand, workers who were oriented to the attainment of a high level of non-economic rewards and a relatively low level of remuneration would tend to select small, low-wage firms.

Furthermore, absenteeism was seen to be not only a response to a depriving work situation, but also a result of the type of relationship between the employee and the organization. Specifically, the level of identification and *moral* involvement of the workers in small firms is likely to reduce absenteeism as the fulfilment of the requirements of the work role is defined by the worker not merely as a part of an economic exchange but as a duty and obligation. In the large plant, the narrowly *calculative* involvement of the worker removes such barriers to absence and in this situation the loss of earnings is the major consideration from the workers' point of view. Thus, the rate of absenteeism in the large plant will be a function of the level of deprivation and the level of the workers' economic wants.

It has been pointed out that it is necessary to demonstrate the independence — relative to the work situation — of these orientations. Two methods of achieving this were outlined. First, it was suggested that direct interview questions might prove useful in assessing the degree of 'self-selection'. Second, various tentative suggestions were put forward for tracing the sources of these differences in orientation to extra-plant factors.

Part II

The Findings

---

6 Some Methodological Considerations

Organizational Size

Most studies of the 'size effect' have neglected to discuss which 'sizes' are important in determining structural changes in organizations; the choice of the sizes to be contrasted seems to have been, in many cases, purely arbitrary. Thus, in previous studies of this problem there is a wide variation in the classification of 'large' and 'small'. For example, Indik's[1] set of 32 package delivery organizations vary in size from 15 to 61 members, the set of 36 automobile sales dealerships from 25 to 132 members and the set of 28 voluntary membership, educational-political organizations from 101 to 2,989 members. The five gasworks used in Revans[2] study varied in size from 67 to 3,430 members and the detailed study presented by the Acton Society Trust[3] in the second of their two reports concerned 12 plants which were classified into three groups: less than 300, 500 to 1,000, and over 3,000.

However, it is possible to argue that the classification of organizational size need not be so arbitrary if it is informed by a rudimentary theoretical framework. The random choice of sizes could only be justified if, in fact, every increase in membership, however small, was accompanied by a *proportionate* structural change — in the form of, say, increased bureaucratization — and the same degree of change in member attachment. This has not been shown and the size-attachment relationship is not so uniform as to suggest that this is the case.

We noted in part I that the level of bureaucratic control of behaviour in industrial organizations is, at least, partly determined by the degree of connectedness in the interaction networks. More precisely, the interaction networks with a high degree of connectedness in the small organizations make it possible for integration to be based upon commonly accepted and internalized norms and customs; whereas, in the large firm the impossibility of realizing all — or, at least, a critical level of the potential interpersonal relationships — means that 'external' control mechanisms, such as standardized rules and regulations, are used. According to Caplow's scheme for classifying organiza-

---

1 Indik, 'Organization Size and Member Participation'.
2 Revans, 'Human Relations, Management and Size'.
3 Acton Society Trust, *Size and Morale*, part II.

tions, which is based on the criterion of interaction possibilities, there are four basic categories:

"The *small* organization is small enough for its members to form a primary group — whether or not they actually do so. Small organizations range from about three to thirty members. The nuclear family is a small organization.

The *medium-size* organization is too large to permit the development of all possible pair relationships among members but it is still small enough so that one or more members, including a leader or leaders, can interact directly with all of the others. The medium-size organization ranges from a minimum membership of about thirty to a maximum of about a thousand.

The *large* organization is too large for any member to know each of the others but not too large for one or more leaders to be recognized by all of the others. These key members will be recognized by many more people than they are able to recognize. The large organization ranges from a lower limit of about one thousand members to an upper limit of fifty thousand, but this upper limit is especially variable. Most universities are large organizations.

The *giant* organization has too many members too widely dispersed to permit the direct interaction of any individual with all of the others. Key members may be recognized by most other members, through mass communications. A lower limit of fifty thousand may be set for the giant organization and there is no upper limit. Political parties are usually giant organizations."[1]

Thus, there are four basic structural types and if the assumptions concerning the relationship between the degree of network connectedness and the level of bureaucratization are correct, then the relationship between size and bureaucratization is not proportionate. Graphically the relationship would be closer to (*a*) than to (*b*) in Figure 3.

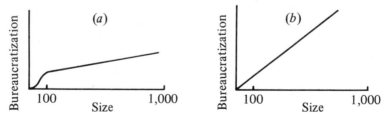

Figure 3. The Relationships between Size and Bureaucratization

1 Theodore Caplow, *Principles of Organization* (New York, 1964), pp. 26-7.

The greatest structural changes (in our case those in the level of bureau-cratization) are likely to occur when an organization reaches about 30 to 60 members and from then on the changes will become smaller until one reaches the largest of the 'large' and the 'giant' organizations. Caplow makes the same point.

> "If a work crew is increased in size from fifteen to thirty, its entire social structure is certain to change because the pattern of primary group interaction cannot be continued intact. A work crew of two hundred men, however, might be doubled in size without any drastic change in its structure."[1]

There are, of course, many reservations to be made about this type of classification and, therefore, about the way in which I have linked this to assumptions concerning the relationship between size and bureaucratization. The main criticism would be that the classification is somewhat arbitrary and this is certainly true; but the virtue of this type of classification is that it is *less* arbitrary than previous methods used in the choice of organizations of different size. Although it is a crude guide, this method points to those groups of organizations that may be meaningfully compared and contrasted in terms of the connectedness of their interaction networks and their level of bureau-cratization. In relation to our present problem it is clear that if an under-standing of the structural features that are important in determining workers' attachment to their organizations is to be gained, then, a sharp contrast of organizational types is needed: one cannot expect to achieve this by con-trasting organizations of 10 members with those of 50, or those of 600 with those of 1,000 or 3,000 members.

Therefore, from the outset it was decided that 'small' was to refer to organizations with less than 100 employees and large to those with over about 3,000 — and the firms were chosen with this in mind.

There was also a second decision — related to the problem of size — to be made in choosing the organizations: whether or not to make the distinction between plant size and firm size. It was finally assumed that a small plant which formed a branch of a larger organization would be likely to be organized more 'bureaucratically' — due to its link with the authority structure of the parent firm — than a small independent organization. There-fore, in order to heighten the contrast, small independent firms were chosen for the small organization group.[2]

---

1 *Ibid*. pp. 25-6.
2 Of course this is not to say that the 'size effect' will not be apparent between branches of different size in the same company.

C

Technology

In part I, chapter 2, it was suggested that technology was the *major* determinant of task specialization in the production system of an industrial organization and it has also been mentioned that technology is an important factor to be taken into consideration when studying the structure of shop floor interaction and the frequency and type of vertical interaction. Furthermore, there is a close relationship between technology and bureaucratization. If we consider Woodward's concept of 'technical complexity' — which refers to the extent to which the production process is controllable and its results predictable then we can see that there is a connection between technical complexity and the level of standardization. That is to say, a controllable and predictable production system will facilitate control of the organization by standardized and formalized means. Thus, technology is of considerable importance as a determinant of worker behaviour. However, it was also suggested that as there is no evidence to indicate that size directly determines technological structure,[1] then the type of technological system must be carefully controlled in the study of the consequences of size for worker attachment. To make the organizations as similar as possible in this respect it was decided to restrict the choice of them to one industry: namely light engineering.

Thus, the organizations were chosen with these two considerations in mind. Locating the large plants presented little difficulty. There were four large plants (over 3,000 employees) to choose from in the Bradford area and the first company I contacted agreed to assist me in the research. The small firms were located by using the local trade telephone directory and writing to a list of randomly selected firms asking the total size of their labour force and whether or not they would be prepared to help in the research. Later, I visited the firms whose managers had agreed to help and explained the project more fully. During the course of these visits I decided that the controls on technology could be implemented by using those organizations with a unit and small batch production systems.[2] At the time I had obtained cooperation from more small firms of this type than any other and, further, the large plant contained a large number of departments with this type of production system. Thus, two small plants were rejected because of their unsuitable mass production technology and two others replaced them.[3]

---

1 See part I, chapter 2.
2 Woodward, *Management and Technology*, pp. 11-13, and *Industrial Organization*, ch. 3.
3 One of these firms was later used in the pilot survey of 15 interviews.

The final number of small firms (eight) was determined by calculating what the population size of respondents would need to be assuming that about 50 workers were to be interviewed and that the non-response was likely to be around 20-25%. As I was planning to deal only with the attachment of skilled and semi-skilled men[1] I required a number of organizations whose aggregates were at least 30 for each skill group.

At a later stage in the research it was decided that it would be useful to compare the plants with a unit and small batch technology with a large plant using a mass production system. In this way it was hoped that, in some crude way at least, a tentative assessment of the independent efforts of technology could be made. The mass production department of the large plant that had already been chosen was unsuitable as it comprised a very high proportion of women in the labour force. Therefore, another plant was used.

Table 6.1 shows the sizes of the organizations that were chosen for the research and describes briefly the types of production systems and products.

After the selection of the industrial organizations the next problem was to select samples of workers, in each type of production system, whose tasks and activities were as similar as possible. These groups of men formed the basis for the interview samples. This strategy was followed in order to match these workers' work situations as closely as possible in all respects but those which it was assumed were a consequence of size. The first step was to include only machinists — that is, turners, millers, borers, drillers, etc. — in the sample. This meant that a small group of fitters in firms *D, E* and *F* were excluded from consideration.

Therefore, these controls meant that the skill levels in *both* the large and small organizations with the unit and small batch technologies were more or less comparable. The skilled men in large plant *A* and those in the small firms are both required to work with technical drawings and have considerable autonomy in the selection of work methods and work pace. Due to the large variety of work a considerable amount of consultation and discussion is required between workers and for similar reasons the borrowing and lending of tools increases the level of required interaction.

This type of production system with its large variety of work also requires that the semi-skilled men in both large and small organizations possess a relatively high degree of skill. In large plant *A* skill status determines the type of machine that can be used. For example, milling and drilling machines are operated by the semi-skilled; whereas skilled workers use lathes and boring machines. This demarcation is a consequence of both national and local trade union agreements but is about the only restriction imposed upon

1 Apprentices, unskilled workers and supervisors were excluded from consideration mainly to restrict the research to manageable proportions.

Table 6.1. Size and Technological Systems of the Organizations
in the Sample

	Size	Unit and small-batch production system
Plant *A* (depts. *x* and *y*)	5,000 (158)	Prototypes of various kinds for use in other branches of the company. Unit and small batches to customers' requirements.
Firm *C*	63	Engineering tools: 'one off' and small batch; also subcontracting.
Firm *D*	26	Textile machinery: machining and assembly; small-batch manufacture of spare parts for the equipment.
Firm *E*	24	Textile machinery: machining and assembly; small-batch manufacture of spare parts for the equipment. Research and development section involved in the construction of prototypes.
Firm *F*	16	Small water and air pumps: small range but also made to customers' requirements.
Firm *G*	12	Subcontracting: small batch and 'one off'.
Firm *H*	9	Subcontracting: small batch and 'one off'.
	Size	Mass production system
Plant *B* (dept. *z*)	3,000 (90)	Mainly motor-car components in long runs. Operatives produce about 1,400 units a day.

the semi-skilled in plant A. The semi-skilled operatives, like the skilled, use measuring instruments throughout their work and are required to do their own setting. The relatively lengthy period of training for semi-skilled men — approximately six months — also suggests that they possess a fairly high degree of skill. The only difference between the semi-skilled in the large plant and those in the small firms is that the absence of unions[1] and union agreements allows the semi-skilled men in the small firms to operate machines that are exclusively the province of the apprentice-trained man in the large unionized plant. However, relatively few semi-skilled workers (about 30%) in the small firms were found to be operating lathes and boring machines; like their counterparts in the large plant they were more often found to be drilling or milling.

In all, firm B comprised about 5,300 workers of which 3,000 were employed in the plant in Bradford which was the object of the research. This plant is engaged primarily in the manufacture of motor-car components. In contrast to the semi-skilled workers in the unit and small batch production systems, the task of the workers in plant B is highly repetitive and standardized with almost no autonomy in methods and very little in pace. The job requires minimum physical movement and no cooperation and consultation. This type of work requires a training period of about two weeks.

The Interview Sample

Plant A

The population in plant A was all male semi-skilled and skilled machinists in departments x and y over the age of 21 who were born in the United Kingdom or Eire. The skilled population numbered 80 and of these a random sample of 40 (1 : 2) was taken: the response was 26 (65%). The semi-skilled population was 58 and of this group a random sample of 29 (1 : 2) was taken: the response here was slightly better at 20 or 69%. The rather low response rate in plant A was partly due to the difficulty in arranging suitable times for meeting those men who worked on the night shift as *all* the interviews were carried out in the respondents' own homes.

Plant B

The total population in plant B comprised all male semi-skilled machinists over the age of 21 who were born in the United Kingdom or Eire. This population numbered 40 and a random sample of 32 was selected: the response proved to be 23 (71.25%).

---

1 Only 3 out of 47 respondents in the small firms were union members, compared with 69 out of 83 in the large plants.

The Small Firms

In the eight small firms the total population of male semi-skilled machinists who were born in the United Kingdom or Eire was 30. All were asked for an interview and 22 agreed (73.2%). The total population of male skilled workers over the age of 21 who were born in the United Kingdom or Eire was 64. In seven of the firms the population was 19 and all of these men were asked for an interview and 12 agreed (63.2%). In firm C the total population of skilled workers was 45. A one in three random sample (that is, 15) was taken and of these 15 men 13 agreed to be interviewed (86.5%).

Therefore, the combined sample was 34, and the response 25 (73.5%).

The five groups of workers that were interviewed are shown below in Table 6.2.

Table 6.2.   Sample Size of Interview Subjects by Organization, Technology and Skill Level

	Small firms: Unit and small-batch technology	Large plant A: Unit and small-batch technology	Large plant B: Mass production technology
Semi-skilled	22	20	23
Skilled	25	26	-

In the case of the large plant workers the interviews[1] were conducted in the respondents' own homes, but for several of the small firm workers the interviews took place in the lunch break at work. The average length of each interview was one hour.

In addition to the samples of workers, several interviews were conducted with the managers in the organizations.

Location of Industry and the Level of Employment

In part I, chapter 1, it was explained that the research was carried out in a single city in order to control labour market variations and consequently to make the labour turnover figures for the various organizations more compar-

1 The interview schedule is to be found in Appendix B.

able. Later, in the theoretical discussion (part I, chapter 3) another reason for this strategy emerged. Briefly, the testing of the 'self-selection' hypothesis is made easier if the workers in question are subject to the same influences concerning the possibility of job changing — that is, the level of employment must be held constant. Furthermore, the level of employment must be high in order to make 'self-selection' and relatively fine discrimination between types of employment a realistic possibility for the worker. At the time the interviewing of the workers was being carried out (May-October 1966) the level of employment in Bradford was high.[1]

---

1 The economic restrictions imposed by the Labour government in the summer of 1966 began to take their effect on plant B (motor-car components) in late October and small reductions in the labour force were made. However, this was not widespread in the industry of the area — for example, plant A announced a large export order and advertised for labour at this time. In June 1966 the unemployment rate for males over the age of 15 was 1.1% for the country as a whole and 0.9% for Bradford.

7 The Structure of Potential Rewards

It was argued in part I that the major structural change brought about by increases in size was that of increasing *bureaucratization*. In this chapter I propose to examine the consequences of varying degrees of bureaucratization for the level and type of non-economic reward in organizations of different size. Here I will be dealing with the specific effects of bureaucratization on the *potential* level of non-economic rewards and not with a general analysis of the bureaucratic form of control.[1] The *actual* levels of reward received by the workers will be dealt with in the next chapter after we have looked also at the differences in levels and types of *expectations from work*.

I have argued earlier that increases in size lead to greater reliance on impersonal modes of control. In other words, the methods by which coordination and cooperation are achieved become standardized and formalized and increasingly rigid; flexibility is reduced as this often entails a loss of predictability of behaviour and thus a loss of managerial control. This type of administrative system develops as direct, interpersonal mechanisms of control become increasingly difficult to implement because of the sheer exigency of size. This reduction in vertical face-to-face interaction is brought about by: increasing spans of managerial control, increases in the number of levels in the managerial hierarchy, and an increase in the managers' potential interaction networks.

First, in part I it was suggested that there is a direct relationship between the number of hierarchical levels, spans of control and size. Evidence for this assertion comes from Haire, Indik and Woodward.[2] Data from the present study conforms to their generalizations. Both large plants had five levels of authority; whereas the small firms had either two or three. Quite simply, this means that there is less chance that the shop floor worker will come into contact with top level management. Perhaps more important in this respect than the number of levels is the size of the *potential interaction networks* of the managerial elite. In the large plants *A* and *B* the potential relationships of the top management are about 5,000 and 3,000 respectively. Even if the managers had need to interact directly with all subordinates this would be a physically impossible task. In the small firms the situation is far different. Apart from the fact that in three of the firms only a foreman held

---

1 This will be dealt with in greater detail in chapter 9.
2 Haire, 'Biological Models'; Indik, 'Relationship between Organization Size and Supervision Ratio'; Woodward, *Management and Technology*.

a position between the chief executive and the shop floor, all the firms were small enough for the owner or managing director to interact with all employees in the course of his instrumental activities.

Even the interaction between the first line supervisor and workers in the large plants will be less frequent than in the small firms due to the greater spans of control in the former. In plants A and B the foremen's spans of control were 21 and 29 respectively; whereas, in the small firms these ranged from 6 to 13 men.

The survey provides evidence for this inverse relationship between size and frequency of vertical interaction. First, all respondents were asked how often they talked to the holder of the managerial position directly above foreman but below other top management. In the large plants this position was referred to as shop supervisor. Only three small firms had a position at this level and in each case the position was that of works manager[1]. The responses to this question are given below in Table 7.1.

Table 7.1. Direct Interaction with Shop Supervisor/Works Manager by Organization and Skill Level

	Small firms: Unit and small-batch technology		Large plant A: Unit and small-batch technology		Large plant B: Mass production technology
	Semi-skilled	Skilled	Semi-skilled	Skilled	Semi-skilled
Talk to shop supervisor/works manager	100%	100%	45%	39%	35%
Do *not* talk to shop supervisor/ works manager	0%	0%	55%	61%	65%
Total %	100%	100%	100%	100%	100%
N	14	20	20	26	23

1 This was of course not the specialized role performed by managers in the large plants. The small firm works managers were also responsible for such functions as sales, personnel, buying, etc.

Even for a large bureaucratized organization it is quite surprising that only between one third and a half of the workers ever spoke to their shop supervisor — especially when one considers the fact that these departments were not themselves very large.[1] A middle level of management was not present in the small firms but in order to complete the picture of the extent of vertical interaction in the large plants the workers were asked if they ever spoke to their *works manager*. We can see from Table 7.2 that in the large organizations management-worker interaction almost ceases after the shop supervisor level.

Table 7.2.   Direct Interaction with Works Manager in Large Plants by Skill Levels

| | Large plant A: Unit and small-batch technology | | Large plant B: Mass production technology |
	Semi-skilled	Skilled	Semi-skilled
Talk to works manager	15%	8%	13%
Do *not* talk to works manager	85%	92%	87%
Total %	100%	100%	100%
N	20	26	23

Finally, the respondents in both types of organization were asked how often they spoke to their *directors* or *managing directors*. In a sense, the comparison between the organizations is not quite legitimate as these roles differ considerably with size. In the small firms the directors are concerned with the production system to a far greater extent than their counterparts in the large organizations. However, the data is instructive in so far as it shows the vast difference between the large and small organizations (Table 7.3).

---

1   70 and 88 in plant A and 90 in plant B.

Table 7.3. Direct Interaction with Director by Size of Organization and Skill Level

	Small firms: Unit and small-batch technology		Large plant A: Unit and small-batch technology		Large plant B: Mass production technology
	Semi-skilled	Skilled	Semi-skilled	Skilled	Semi-skilled
Talk to director	95%	96%	0%	4%	0%
Do *not* talk to director	5%	4%	100%	96%	100%
Total %	100%	100%	100%	100%	100%
N	22	25	20	26	23

As I have frequently stressed, the consequences of this wide variation in the frequency of management-worker interaction are not merely, as Indik would seem to suggest[1], to influence the degree to which vertical relations are characterized by affect. The consequences are more far reaching than that. As I suggested in part I, a high frequency of vertical interaction in a small organization — or more accurately, a situation in which management is able to interact with all or nearly all subordinates — provides a basis for the development of a control system which is founded upon commonly accepted norms. Also the highly connected networks on the shop floor will facilitate the spread and acceptance of these norms. Conversely, this is impossible in the large organization, therefore delegation of authority and control on the basis of standardized and formalized rules and regulations is necessary. It must also be noted that the relationship between vertical interaction and the level of bureaucratization is reciprocal; that is to say, a high level of standardization and formalization in an organization will tend to reduce further the frequency of face-to-face interaction as standardized procedure becomes a functional alternative for this process.[2]

1 Indik, 'Some Effects of Organization Size on Member Attitudes and Behaviour'.
2 Gouldner, *Patterns of Industrial Bureaucracy*.

We must now turn to those consequences of variations in bureaucratization that have been shown by previous research to be important in the structuring of non-economic rewards in work. These were briefly discussed in part I under the heads: (i) the structuring of work tasks, (ii) shop-floor interaction, (iii) authority relationships. The main comparisons and contrasts will, of course, be made between the technologically similar organizations, but at most stages contrasts will be made with the technologically different large plant B in order to stress certain points in the argument. This method will also − in a crude way − enable us to consider the relative importance of size and technology in the analysis of the level of potential rewards from work.

(i) The Structuring of Task Rewards

I have previously argued that, although technology is the major determinant of task specialization in the system of production, size, through its influence on the level of bureaucratization, may exert some influence in this direction. And further, that the level of task specialization is inversely related to the level of potential rewards from the work activity. It was argued that large organizations are faced with the problem of controlling the work process and the labour force's instrumental activities in a situation where informal 'custom' can only become operative in small work groups or, at most, in certain departments within the organization. In this situation standardized procedure facilitates the 'remote control', by management, of the work process. It is usual in this type of system for 'spheres of competence' to be rigidly demarcated. Whatever 'official' job rotation there may be, 'informal' rotation is not sanctioned as this entails a loss of managerial control.[1] Furthermore, the worker in the large organization is also likely to be subject to more bureaucratic constraints in the form of union rules governing manning and demarcation. We have already seen that workers in the large plant A with the unit and small batch system are restricted in this way in the number of different types of machine they are allowed to operate.

---

1 This is not to say that informal custom within certain sections or groups is not carried out; nor am I suggesting that this may not be a more 'efficient' system. What I am trying to do is to identify the major features of two different types of control system: namely, those of large and small industrial organizations. In this respect I entirely agree with Gouldner's statement to the effect that the Weberian tradition of organizational analysis, although it tends to neglect the 'informal' in organizations, concentrates on those very aspects that distinguish the modern organization. A. W. Gouldner, 'Organizational Analysis', in R. K. Merton (ed.), *Sociology Today* (New York, 1959), pp. 400-27.

In the small organizations, informally developed norms and customs can become the basis for the control of the instrumental activities in the production system. For example, a managing director in one of the small firms stated that he expected his workers to be able to carry on production with little or no direct supervision or official directives — that is to say, within the limits imposed by technology, the workers in the small firms possessed a great deal of autonomy in the production process. One consequence of this less standardized system is that workers are rarely restricted to one job or machine. In the course of conversations with workers and management, it emerged that men in the small firms would take a partly finished product to another machine to complete the whole process rather than leave it for the next man if he were busy. Furthermore, as was suggested in part I, job rotation of this kind was strongly encouraged by the management and the reasons for this would seem to stem from the exigencies posed by small scale. In a small firm of 25 employees the absence or quitting of one of two 'key' workers can disrupt the process of production to a far greater extent than in the large plant. The absence of a single man in the small firm could mean that a whole link — e.g. milling — in production might be broken; whereas, in the large firm it is unlikely that absence in one department could be of such a scale as to cause the system to break down. Thus, it is important that small firms have labour forces with a variety of skills and a knowledge of the whole production process in order that adaptation can occur in disruptive situations of the kind described above. In such small firms the more rigid bureaucratic mode of control would undoubtedly be less effective.[1] As we have already seen, the absence of union organization in all the small firms in the present sample means that further restrictions on job rotation are lifted.

The actual amount and frequency of job rotation in the organizations can be estimated from the answers to the question: "Do you ever move from your usual machine?" "How often is this?" (Table 7.4).

As expected, the level of job rotation is higher in the small firms than in either of the large plants. Also in line with expectation is the very low level of rotation produced by a high level of bureaucratization and the mass production technology in plant B. Thus, the data suggest that the level of potential task rewards is higher in the small firms due to the less formally administered work process.

---

1 See Arthur L. Stinchcombe, 'Bureaucratic and Craft Administration of Production: A Comparative Study', *Administrative Science Quarterly*, vol. 4 (1959).

Table 7.4.   Amount and Frequency of Job Rotation by Size of Organization and Skill Level

	Small firms: Unit and small-batch technology		Large plant A: Unit and small-batch technology		Large plant B: Mass production technology
	Semi-skilled	Skilled	Semi-skilled	Skilled	Semi-skilled
Moves from machine more than *weekly*	64%	64%	25%	11%	22%
Moves from machine once every one or two *months*	18%	16%	10%	23%	0%
Never moves from machine	18%	20%	65%	66%	78%
Total %	100%	100%	100%	100%	100%
N	22	25	20	26	23

(ii) Shop-floor Interaction

Briefly, the argument in this respect is that size, through its influence on the level of bureaucratization, influences in a negative direction, both the frequency of interaction and the degree of network connectedness in an organization. Further, the frequency of interaction and the degree of network connectedness are directly related to the level of potential rewards from peer relations.

We have already mentioned that technology is important in structuring interaction in an industrial organization and data in this section will show that a combination of a high level of bureaucratization and a mass production technology (plant B), which needs little 'required' interaction and which limits 'optional'[1] interaction, produces the lowest level of shop-floor interaction of

1   See part II, chapter 6, for a description of the technologies and the limits imposed upon social interaction.

any of the organizations that were studied. The major comparisons in this section will be between the organizations with the unit and small batch technologies in which there is a relatively high level of 'required' interaction. Bureaucratization affects both the levels of 'required' and 'optional' interaction. On the one hand, the job rotation in the small firms has the effect of increasing 'required' interaction and, in turn, the degree of connectedness in the interaction network; whereas, the more rigid demarcation in the large plants tends to restrict 'required' interaction. On the other hand, both large plants possessed rules which were designed specifically to prohibit off-the-job ('optional') interaction. In the case of large plant A, with the unit and small batch technology that demands some interaction, this regulation was more difficult to enforce than in plant B. Furthermore, the more 'rationally' organized production systems in the large plants left little time for breaks between jobs which workers could use for conversation with work mates. The greater degree of control of the production system exercised by the workers themselves in the small firms meant that they were, to some degree, controllers of the frequency of breaks between jobs. This contrasts sharply with the 'externally' imposed disciplines of the production engineers' schedules in the large plants. This point can be illustrated by the data in Table 7.5 which shows the reported frequency of breaks between jobs.

Table 7.5.   Reported Frequency of Breaks between Jobs by Size of Organization and Skill Level

	Small firms: Unit and small-batch technology		Large plant A: Unit and small-batch technology		Large plant B: Mass production technology
	Semi-skilled	Skilled	Semi-skilled	Skilled	Semi-skilled
'regularly'/ 'occasionally'	73%	88%	20%	31%	9%
'rarely'/ 'never'	27%	12%	80%	69%	91%
Total %	100%	100%	100%	100%	100%
N	22	25	20	26	23

An indication of the frequency of shop-floor interaction can be gathered from the following tables — 7.6 and 7.7. First, the respondents were asked which alternative — 'a great deal', 'now and then', or 'hardly ever' — described most accurately how often they talked to their work mates.

Table 7.6.   Reported Frequency of Shop Floor Interaction by Size of Organization and Skill Level

	Small firms: Unit and small-batch technology		Large plant A: Unit and small-batch technology		Large plant B: Mass production technology
	Semi-skilled	Skilled	Semi-skilled	Skilled	Semi-skilled
'a great deal'	73%	60%	55%	27%	17%
'now and then'	27%	40%	45%	54%	43%
'hardly ever'	0%	0%	0%	19%	40%
Total %	100%	100%	100%	100%	100%
N	22	25	20	26	23

Table 7.7.   Reported Frequency of Shop Floor Interaction by Size of Organization and Skill Level

	Small firms: Unit and small-batch technology		Large plant A: Unit and small-batch technology		Large plant B: Mass production technology
	Semi-skilled	Skilled	Semi-skilled	Skilled	Semi-skilled
'all the time'/ over 6 times per day	77%	68%	65%	42%	26%
3 or 4 times per day/once or twice per day	23%	32%	35%	58%	74%
Total %	100%	100%	100%	100%	100%
N	22	25	20	26	23

In order to eliminate distortion in the workers' estimates of the frequency of interaction that might stem from different perceptions of 'a great deal', etc., in systems where the frequency of interaction differs the respondents were also asked to specify, as accurately as possible, how many *times* per day they spoke to their fellow workers. The results in Table 7.7 show the same relative differences between organizations and skill levels as the data in Table 7.6. That is to say, in both sets of data the small firms show the highest level of interaction and the large mass production plant the lowest.

Data on *when* the interaction takes place are useful in assessing how far the interaction is 'required' or 'optional' off-the-job. In this respect size appears to make less difference than technology. In the technologically similar organizations – large plant A and the small firms – the majority of workers report interaction 'at any time at all'; whereas, in large plant B 65% of the workers report interaction 'only' or 'mostly' at break time. (Table 7.8)

Table 7.8.   Time When Interaction Occurs by Size of Organization and Skill Level

| | Small firms: Unit and small-batch technology | | Large plant A: Unit and small-batch technology | | Large plant B: Mass production technology |
	Semi-skilled	Skilled	Semi-skilled	Skilled	Semi-skilled
'only at break time'	5%	0%	0%	0%	17%
'Mostly at break time'	5%	12%	15%	42%	48%
'at any time at all'	90%	88%	85%	58%	35%
Total %	100%	100%	100%	100%	100%
N	22	25	20	26	23

Thus, size of organization appears to be inversely related to both opportunities for, and the frequency of, shop floor interaction. We can, therefore, conclude that, *ceteris paribus*, size is inversely related to the potential level of rewards from social relationships with peers.

(iii) Authority Relationships

We have already seen, in the analysis of some of the determinants of bureaucratization, that levels of management-worker interaction vary inversely with size of organization. Thus, potential rewards stemming from relationships with superiors are at a far higher level in the small firms. In the large plants management-worker interaction almost ceases above the level of shop supervisor. Here, I wish to continue the argument by referring to the differences in norms typically governing these role relationships in the two types of organization. In the large industrial organization authority relationships are typified by *universalistic* norms in order to regulate *specific instrumental* relationships and activities. On the other hand, I hope to show that the authority relationships of the small organization are marked by a greater degree of *particularism* and that the relationships are more *diffuse*.[1]

Universalism/Particularism

First, I must stress that I am dealing with cases in which the norms governing all types of authority relationships are basically universalistic; the element of particularism to be found in the small firms is only a minor and secondary pattern. However, this does not mean that it is relatively unimportant; on the contrary, particularism in the situation typified by contract and the 'cash nexus' has important consequences.

I should like to illustrate this contrast in norms by reference to the differences in the way the 'grievance procedure' is administered in the two types of organization in question. The 'grievance procedure' of both large plants were standardized and common to all cases. These were a combination of company policy and union agreements. In plant *A* the formal procedure is as follows: the grievance is first taken to a foreman and if it is not settled at this stage it is then taken to the shop steward. A failure to agree means that the problem is then taken to the chief shop steward and higher level management. At this stage, if there is still no solution, outside negotiators from the union and the Employers' Federation are brought in and the problem may, in fact, reach the monthly union conference (A.E.U.) at York. The procedure in plant *B* is very similar. In informal interviews, managers at both large plants were asked if they considered it more important, in dealing with grievances, to take into account what they knew about the persons involved or whether they preferred to deal with them according to previous rulings on similar

---

1 Talcott Parsons, *The Social System* (London, 1951).

cases. Most agreed that it was "helpful to know" the people involved, but also stated that this approach was impossible to use in a large company. They all stressed that company rulings must be *followed*.

In none of the small firms was there any standardized procedure for dealing with grievances and other such problems. These were usually sorted out by an informal talk between the workers and the managing director and, furthermore, the management and the owners in the small firms all thought it more important to take into account knowledge about the individuals involved even at the expense of consistency in the treatment of workers' problems.

Specificity/Diffuseness

Again it must be noted that differences between the organizations, with respect to these norms, are not absolute. In all industrial organizations workers are brought together for a limited and *specific* purpose. However, in the small firm, other aspects of interpersonal relationships apart from those necessary for the industrial situation are brought into authority relationships to an extent which is impossible in the large plant.

First, I will illustrate the argument with data taken from the survey in which I will take the *content* of vertical interaction as an indicator of the levels of specificity and diffuseness in the authority relationships. On the one hand, a high proportion of *work-centred* conversations will be taken to indicate a high level of specificity; on the other hand, a high level of *non*-work-centred conversation will be considered to be an indicator of an element of diffuseness in the relationship. Second, less systematic data taken from conversations with managers and workers will be used to illustrate the same argument.

All respondents were asked how often they talked to their foreman about things *other* than work, and the data, which show clearly that the worker-foreman relationship in the large plants is far more specific than in the small firms, are given in Table 7.9.

Of course, the differences in this respect become more marked when worker/high-level management interaction is considered. When questioned about the frequency of direct interaction between themselves and shop supervisors, works managers and directors or others, the workers were also asked *what* they talked about. Three codes were used in the analysis of these data and a word of explanation about these is necessary. Those workers who mentioned exclusively work-centred conversations were then asked if they ever talked about anything else; whereas, those who mentioned non-work subjects first were immediately coded as mentioning 'non-work

Table 7.9. Frequency of Non-work Conversation with Foreman by Size of Organization and Skill Level

	Small firms: Unit and small-batch technology		Large plant *A*: Unit and small-batch technology		Large plant *B*: Mass production technology
	Semi-skilled	Skilled	Semi-skilled	Skilled	Semi-skilled
Non-work conversation at least *once a day*	55%	56%	20%	15%	4%
Non-work conversation *several* times per *week*	45%	28%	15%	19%	26%
Non-work conversation *less* than *weekly* or *never*	0%	16%	65%	66%	70%
Total %	100%	100%	100%	100%	100%
N	22	25	20	26	23

spontaneously' and asked no other questions. That is to say, it was assumed that work was the basis of interaction and the question was designed to assess how far non-work aspects were involved. As in Table 7.1 the authority level directly above foreman in each organization is taken for comparison. The figures in Table 7.10 show that for the majority of the 40% or so in the large plants who do report interaction with their head of department, the relationship is highly specific and concerned with the organization's instrumental activities. The data from the small firms show the the contrast: of the two skill levels *all* report some interaction and only 14% of the semi-skilled report only work-centred conversations.

Above this level in the managerial hierarchy no meaningful comparisons can be made as *only one worker* in the large plants reported interaction with the managing directors. However, an examination of the data from the small firms only is helpful as they show the extent to which non-work elements enter into the relationships between owners and workers (Table 7.11).

84

Table 7.10. Content of Shop Supervisor/Works Manager-worker Interaction by Size of Organization and Skill Level

	Small firms: Unit and small-batch technology		Large plant A: Unit and small-batch technology		Large plant B: Mass production technology
	Semi-skilled	Skilled	Semi-skilled	Skilled	Semi-skilled
No interaction with shop supervisor/works manager	0%	0%	55%	62%	66%
Work *only*	14%	0%	35%	22%	26%
Non-work mentioned spontaneously	22%	40%	0%	0%	4%
Total %	100%	100%	100%	100%	100%
N^*	14	20	20	26	23

$*N$ = number of respondents in those firms with a works manager.

Other indications that the authority relationships in the small firms are more diffuse come from statements made by workers and managers. For example, in one small firm the owners played dominoes and cards with the workers at lunch time in the canteen and two workers said that they had been to the owners' homes on informal visits. In another firm the owner often lent money to his employees to help them in buying a house.

Therefore in small firms, rewards in the form of 'personalized' authority relationships are potentially obtainable by the worker. In certain cases the rewards received may stem from 'status enhancement' due to association with persons of higher status. In the large plants such rewards are almost entirely absent. In fact, the impersonality — that is, the universalism and specificity in the role relationship — is a potential source of dissatisfaction.

Table 7.11.   Content of Managing Director/Owner-worker Interaction in the Small Firms by Skill Level

	Small firms: Unit and Small-batch technology	
	Semi-skilled	Skilled
No interaction with directors/owners	5%	4%
Work *only*	5%	0%
Work *and non*-work (after probe)	50%	48%
Non-work mentioned spontaneously	40%	48%
Total %	100%	100%
N	22	25

(iv) The Level of Economic Rewards

As I mentioned in part I, large differences were found in the wages paid by the organizations in the sample. Tables 7.12 and 7.13 show the average *gross* weekly earnings of the skilled and semi-skilled men in the sample. The date were collected during the period December 1965-February 1966.

Table 7.12.   Skilled Workers' Gross Average Weekly Earnings

	Size	40-hour week			With overtime, bonus, etc.		
		£	*s.*	*d.*	£	*s.*	*d.*
Plant *A**	5,000	19	11	-	21	10	-
*B**	3,000	17	16	-	20	plus	-
Firm *C*+	63	15	10	-	17	10	-
D	26	14	10	-	17	10	-
E	24	14	10	-	16	10	-
F	16	14	10	-	16	-	-
G‡	12	14	10	-	16	-	-
H†	9	15	-	-	16	-	-

Table 7.13.   Semi-skilled Workers' Gross Average Weekly Earnings

	Size	40-hour week			With overtime, bonus, etc.		
		£	s.	d.	£	s.	d.
Plant A	5,000	16	12	-	18	10	-
B	3,000	16	10	-	19	10	-
Firm C⁺	63	12	10	-	13	5	-
D	26	11	-	-	13	10	-
E	24	13	-	-	14	10	-
F	16	11	10	-	12	-	-
G‡	12	14	10	-	16	-	-
H‡	9	15	-	-	16	-	-

* The skilled workers in plant *B* were not interviewed.

⁺ The figures for the small firms are averages as there are differences of up to 30s. per week between the wages *within* the skill levels of a single firm. All but one of the owners of a small firm said that they paid a man according to their assessment of his worth.

‡ In these firms there were no differences between the wages of the two skill levels.

Clearly then, the earnings of the workers in the large plants are far higher than those of their counterparts in the small firms.

Thus, with respect to the levels and types of reward in the two kinds of organization, we have a situation in which the small firms are, potentially, the source of a high level of non-economic reward and a relatively low level of remuneration; whereas, the large plants offer lower potential non-economic rewards and substantially higher remuneration. The two large plants differ in their type of technology and thus there are relatively wide differences in their potential levels of non-economic rewards; especially with respect to work task rewards.

8 Expectations, Rewards and Deprivations from Work

WANTS AND EXPECTATIONS FROM WORK

In part I it was hypothesized that workers who were oriented to the attainment of high earnings would tend to select the large, high wage plants for employment. Within this group of workers there are likely to be variations in the degree to which non-economic 'wants' are important considerations in job choice. It was suggested that, on the one hand, some workers may value non-economic rewards in work but that in a situation where the attainment of both high earnings and non-economic rewards was not possible, they would tend to give priority to their economic wants and sacrifice the possibility of non-economic rewards. On the other hand, it is likely that some groups of workers do not especially value or expect a high level of non-economic rewards in work. Both these types of worker were referred to as having an *economistic-instrumental* orientation to work. Similarly, it was hypothesized that workers whose economic wants were at a relatively low level and who were oriented to the attainment of a high level of non-economic rewards (especially task rewards and to a lesser extent social rewards from peer relationships) would tend to select the small, low-wage firms for employment. This orientation was termed *non-economic-expressive*.

Thus, the present problem is (*a*) to demonstrate that wide variations in expectations from work exist, and (*b*) to attempt to show how far such expectations have been involved in determining the job choices of the workers in question.

All the respondents in the sample were asked: "Supposing you were looking for a job what would be your most important consideration?" If the respondent answered that economic considerations (wages and/or security) were most important he was then asked: "Would you look for anything else?" Similarly, if non-economic considerations were mentioned first the same probe was made. Thus, this method gave four alternative responses: economic considerations only; economic considerations (first choice) plus non-economic considerations (after probe); non-economic considerations (first choice) plus economic considerations (after probe); non-economic considerations only. The results yielded by this question are shown below in Table 8.1.

From these data one can see quite clearly that the workers in the small firms do, in fact, consider that non-economic rewards are very important

Table 8.1.   Considerations in Job Choice by Size of Organization and
Skill Level

	Small firms: Unit and small-batch technology		Large plant A: Unit and small-batch technology		Large plant B: Mass production technology
	Semi-skilled	Skilled	Semi-skilled	Skilled	Semi-skilled
Economic considerations only	9%	4%	65%	54%	74%
Economic (1st choice) plus non-economic (after probe)	41%	32%	25%	19%	26%
Non-economic (1st choice) plus economic (after probe)	18%	25%	5%	19%	0%
Non-economic considerations only	32%	40%	5%	8%	0%
Total %	100%	100%	100%	100%	100%
N	22	25	20	26	23

in choosing a job – 91% of the semi-skilled and 96% of the skilled fall into
this category. What is, perhaps, surprising is the fact that large numbers of
workers in the small firms – 32% of the semi-skilled and 40% of the skilled –
mentioned *only* non-economic factors. This, of course, does not suggest that
they would work in the firm of their choice regardless of the level of pay;
but it does show the way in which economic considerations assume little
importance once a basic minimum wage has been found. Many of the workers
from the small firms answered this question in what can only be described as
an embarrassed way. It was as if they were conscious of their 'non-rational'
behaviour in a situation whose institutionalized norms demanded economic

'rationality'. Some workers felt obliged to explain their response:

> "Some people would say the money but for me it's secondary. You may think this is funny, but we must enjoy our work as we spend one third of our lives there."

> "This may sound silly, but I would rather enjoy my work than go for the money."

> "It would not be for the money — I would look for better work and definitely not in a big place...where you are just a number."

> "I would look for a small firm — I don't want to get lost in a big organization despite the money."

In contrast, the workers in the large plants often answered this question with expressions of incredulity — "money, of course" was the common reply.

If we break down the non-economic category in Table 8.1 this will give us an indication of those non-economic rewards which are considered to be most important by the workers (Table 8.2).

The data in Table 8.2 demonstrates that of those workers whose expectations from work are of the non-economic kind, regardless of the importance attached to economic rewards, the large majority consider interesting work to be the most important. However, a substantial minority in the small firms (but nobody in the large plants) stated that the nature of the social relationships at work were an important consideration in job choice. These data and conclusions support the suggestion, made in part I, that major considerations in job choice would be directed to the immediate features of the work situation — that is, to remuneration and the kind of activity involved in the work task. Two arguments may be put forward as an explanation for this. First, social relationships at work are usually valued less than those in out-plant situations, such as the family or freely chosen friendship group. Second, social interaction at work — at least amongst peers — will usually be of an affective kind (however superficial) wherever technological circumstances permit. Therefore, a minimum level of 'social rewards' will comprise a 'given' in wants and expectations from work. The minority of workers in the small firms who did mention that friendly social relationships were an important consideration would appear to be looking for a level of affectivity in such relationships over and above this usual 'minimum'. Their choices of a small firm for employment were obviously made with these considerations in mind.

Table 8.2.   Type of Non-economic Considerations in Job Choice by Size
of Organization and Skill Level

	Small firms: Unit and small-batch technology		Large plant A: Unit and small-batch technology		Large plant B: Mass production technology
	Semi-skilled	Skilled	Semi-skilled	Skilled	Semi-skilled
Interesting work	73%	56%	25%	34%	13%
Friendly social relationships*	14%	28%	0%	0%	0%
Other, e.g. clean not heavy, etc.	4%	12%	10%	12%	13%
Economic considerations only	9%	4%	65%	54%	74%
Total %	100%	100%	100%	100%	100%
N	22	25	20	26	23

* The responses do not allow a distinction to be made between peer and
authority relationships. Those who considered the nature of the social
relationships to be an important consideration replied with such answers
as: "I would like a nice friendly shop." Indeed, it is likely that such
workers do not, themselves, make such a distinction.

The variations in the level of economic wants between the workers in the
different size organizations can be further illustrated by the data in Figure 4
below. The respondents were asked if they would be prepared to leave their
present employment for another firm if in doing this, and working the *same*
number of hours and doing the *same job*, they could earn 10s. a week more.
If the respondent answered 'no' then the 'offer' was increased to 15s., then to
£1 and so on up to £4 or until the worker stated that he would not leave for
any amount. We can see from the results that, despite their high wages, the
workers in the large plants are still sensitive to relatively small increases in
earnings. In plant A 43% and in plant B 66% said that they would be prepared
to leave their present employment for £1 or less; only 2% in the small firms

expressed a willingness to leave for the same amounts. Without prompting, many workers in the small firms referred explicitly to the way in which the receipt of non-economic rewards had to be balanced against the level of remuneration in any decision regarding the changing of jobs; for example: "Three pounds would not be enough – friendship counts for a lot."

Figure 4. Willingness to Change Firm for Higher Wages
(Cumulative Percentage Distribution)

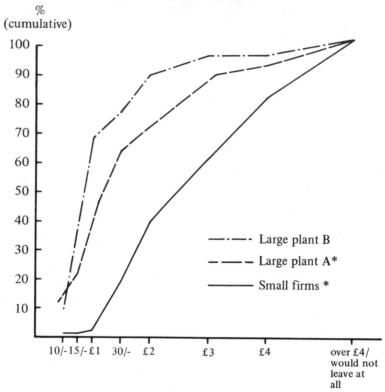

* As there are only very few small variations between the skill levels within the different organizations the different skill level groups have been combined in order to make for clearer reading.

The next problem, after demonstrating that variations in expectations do exist, is to show that these wants and expectations were involved in the workers' choices of their present employment.

Quite simply, we can consider, to begin with, the workers' expressed reasons for choosing their present employment. First, the workers were asked to give their reasons for leaving their last job (Table 8.3).

Table 8.3.   Reasons for Leaving Last Job by Size of Organization and
Skill Level

	Small firms: Unit and small-batch technology		Large plant A: Unit and small-batch technology		Large plant B: Mass production technology
	Semi-skilled	Skilled	Semi-skilled	Skilled	Semi-skilled
Non-economic:					
Boring work	41%	30%	5%	0%	0%
Unfriendly shop	5%	13%	9%	0%	0%
Bad/unfriendly management	9%	4%	5%	0%	0%
Economic:					
Poor pay	18%	13%	35%	50%	65%
Insecure/disliked payment system	0%	0%	0%	8%	9%
Don't know/ vague/involuntary moves	27%	23%	32%	37%	22%
Bad physical conditions	0%	17%	14%	0%	4%
Total %	100%	100%	100%	100%	100%
N*	22	23	22	19	23

*N = the number of responses of those workers who had worked elsewhere.

The majority of workers in the small firms left their previous employment
because of the inadequate level of non-economic rewards. Of these non-
economic rewards those concerned with the task itself once again appear to
be the most important from the workers' point of view. In plant A, the
majority of responses refer to what these more economistic and instrumental

workers considered to be poor pay in their last jobs. A minority of workers (19%) in the semi-skilled group gave reasons which referred to the unsatisfactory level of non-economic rewards. In plant B poor pay was almost the sole reason for voluntary moves. Second, the respondents were asked if there was "anything special" about their present firm that had prompted them to go there for a job. The proportions of each group who answered 'yes' are shown below in Table 8.4.

Table 8.4.   Percentage of Workers attracted to their Firm by 'Something Special'

	Small firms: Unit and small-batch technology		Large plant A: Unit and small-batch technology		Large plant B: Mass production technology
	Semi-skilled	Skilled	Semi-skilled	Skilled	Semi-skilled
Attracted to present firm by "something special"*	41%	52%	35%	39%	61%
N	22	25	20	26	23

* The relatively low proportion of workers answering 'yes' to this question could be interpreted as evidence of the fact that job choice is not so precise and 'rational' a process as I have suggested. However, subsequent data do show that the large majority of workers are aware of conditions in the labour market and the range of alternatives open to them. The low positive response to this question is, I believe, due to the inadequacy of the question itself. It would appear that "something special" was interpreted by the respondents as meaning 'special' as opposed to usual and normal considerations.

The most important fact from the point of view of the present argument is that there are wide variations in the workers' definitions of "something special". Table 8.5 shows the content of these "definitions".

Table 8.5. Definition of 'Something Special' by Size of Organization and Skill Level

	Small firms: Unit and small-batch technology		Large plant A: Unit and small-batch technology		Large plant B: Mass production technology
	Semi-skilled	Skilled	Semi-skilled	Skilled	Semi-skilled
High wages	0%	0%	100%	90%	100%
Interesting work	44%	53%	0%	0%	0%
Small firm social relationships	44%	40%	0%	0%	0%
Near home	12%	7%	0%	10%	0%
Total %	100%	100%	100%	100%	100%
N	9	13	7	10	14

Thus, for half the respondents in the small firms the special reason was the interesting type of work. For a further 40% — that is, about 20% of the total number of workers in the small firms — the friendly and informal social relationships of a small firm were the reason for choosing their present employment. For example:

> "I had heard it was more of a family concern which meant personal contact with the boss — I like to know what he wants and then I can give it to him."

This question of size was brought up by the respondents without prompting. For workers in the large plants "something special" unequivocally meant high wages.

It could of course be argued that workers continue their employment in small firms because they are unaware of the fact that high wages can be got in large plants. Parnes,[1] on the basis of his own and previous research on labour

1 H. S. Parnes, *Research on Labour Mobility* (New York, 1954).

mobility in America, concluded that only a *minority* of workers have an 'adequate' knowledge of the labour market. In the present case, the fact that some of the small firms were situated only a few hundred yards away from the large, high wage plants would lead one to suspect such an interpretation. In fact, evidence from the survey shows that the *large majority* of the workers in the small firms know of the high wages in the other companies of the area. All the respondents were asked if they could name engineering firms in the Bradford area which paid more than their own for a *similar* job and the *same* number of hours. Sixty-four per cent of the semi-skilled and 92% of the skilled men in the small firms were able to do this accurately.[1] Obviously, far fewer workers in the large, high wage plants were able to do this, but it is interesting to note that those who did (20% of the semi-skilled and 12% of the skilled in plant *A*, and 4% in plant *B*) made very fine distinction between various wage rates and hours in the large plants in the area. This suggests that they were taking even minor differences into consideration and displaying a highly economistic orientation to work.

The workers in the small firms who could name organizations with higher wages than their own were then asked *why* they did not go for the high wages. The responses (Table 8.6) of those workers show clearly the strength of their expressive orientation to work and also that the model of a 'rational'

Table 8.6.   Reasons for Small Firm Workers' Reluctance to go to High Wage Plants by Skill Level

	Small firms: Unit and small-batch technology	
	Semi-skilled	Skilled
Poor quality of work/'don't like piecework'/'rather do a good job'	50%	35%
Too big/too impersonal	29%	44%
Too far to travel/too old	14%	4%
Don't know/vague/other reasons	7%	17%
Total %	100%	100%
N	14	23

1 The accuracy of these statements was easy to check as most respondents referred to the large plants of this study. Another plant was frequently cited and information on wages was gathered for comparison.

worker weighing 'net advantages' is, contrary to the views of those who stress elements of randomness in labour mobility, adequate, at least in the present case, for the analysis of worker behaviour.

The main considerations that were involved in the decision not to go to the high wage plants concerned the type of work and payment system and the impersonal nature of the large organizations. Many of the respondents knew that the tasks in the high wage plants would enable them to use their skills, but complained that the piecework times would prevent them from performing the tasks to their own high standards of quality. A desire to escape becoming 'just another number', 'a handle on a machine', or 'just another face' kept the men in the small firms. Many of the respondents were, in fact, informed by experience in the large plants of this study and in all 41% of the semi-skilled and 52% of the skilled men had worked, at some time, in large plants in the area.

The data have shown that wide variations in wants and expectations from work do exist between the workers in the large and small organizations. The majority of workers in the small firms were seen to be oriented to the attainment of a high level of reward from the activity of work itself. A smaller number consider that the social relationships of the work situation — both peer and authority relationships — to be the most important non-economic reward. I have not, of course, suggested that workers with this *non-economistic-expressive* orientation are prepared to pursue these goals without reference to remuneration. Rather, it would appear that these workers set their economic wants at a relatively low level and are, therefore, able to fulfil their non-economic requirements in the type of situation in question here. The orientations of the workers in the large plants are more narrowly *economistic* and *instrumental*; that is, these workers are oriented to the attainment of high earnings and give little importance to non-economic rewards. A minority of these workers were seen to value task rewards also, but this was only very rarely put before economic wants in their scale of priorities (see Tables 8.1 and 8.2). Furthermore, it is significant that no respondent from the large plant groups mentioned that rewarding social relationships were an important requirement in employment.

Moreover, we saw that these variations in orientation to work resulted in the workers' making different types of choices in their selection of employment. The majority of the workers in the large plants had left their previous employment because of what they considered to be poor pay and had chosen their present organizations because of the high level of remuneration they offered. On the other hand, the workers in the small firms had given priority to non-economic factors in their job choices. In short, the 'self-selection' hypothesis has proved to be a useful one.

D

REWARDS AND DEPRIVATIONS IN WORK

In this second part of the chapter I propose to show the variations in the levels and types of reward and deprivation as these are *experienced* by the workers in the large and small organizations. However, before doing this a word is necessary about the concept of rewards. The main data to be used in this discussion come from the responses to the question: "What do you most like about working at your present firm?" Answers to this question point to those features of the work situation that form the most salient rewards from the worker's point of view; but this is not the same as 'satisfaction'. For example, a worker may find the task highly *rewarding* but he may be *dissatisfied* because of a very high level of expectation.[1] In some respects, this method of questioning has certain advantages over the forced choice satisfaction questions.[2] Most important is the fact that it allows the respondent to suggest which aspect of the situation he finds most rewarding. Forced choice questions may give precision but often lead to the worker's giving a statement about an aspect of his work which has no importance for him and is, therefore, not very useful in assessing the likely determinants of his behaviour.[3]

Similarly, the level of deprivation is assessed mainly by referring to the answers to the question: "What do you dislike most about working at your present firm?" The relationship between deprivation and dissatisfaction is less ambiguous. That is to say, it is unlikely that people can express satisfaction with something they view as depriving; whereas it is possible to be dissatisfied with something that is viewed as rewarding.

The discussion is arranged under four heads: task rewards; social rewards from peer relationships; social rewards from authority relationships; and economic rewards. In other words, the following analysis is organized in the same way as that of chapter 2 which dealt with the structure of *potential* rewards.

(i) Task Rewards

In chapter 2 we saw that, within the limits imposed by the production

---

1 Indik, for example ('Organization size and member participation'), does not note this distinction. He uses questions in which respondents are asked to choose between alternatives such as 'I like it very much' or 'I don't like it at all', but classified the responses as indicators of satisfaction.

2 For example, questions which ask the respondents to choose between alternatives which vary from, say, 'very satisfied' to 'very dissatisfied'.

3 Of course, there is always a problem in attempting to make inferences about conduct from observations of attitudes. See P. S. Cohen, 'Social Attitudes and Sociological Enquiry', *British Journal of Sociology*, vol. 17 (1966).

systems, organizational size was directly related to task specialization which is, in turn, inversely related to rewards stemming from the performance of the work task. Data, from the responses to the question: "What do you most like about working at your present firm?" support this proposition. In the small firms, 37% of the semi-skilled and 27% of the skilled men reported that they found the task itself the most rewarding aspect of their employment. In large plant *A* 15% of the semi-skilled and 12% of the skilled gave this response. Significantly, no worker reported rewards from the relatively repetitive and monotonous tasks of the mass production system in operation in plant *B*.

Conversely, answers that refer to boredom and lack of variety in work in response to the question: "What do you dislike most about working at your present firm?" were given *only* by workers in the large plants. In large plant *A* 10% of the semi-skilled and 4% of the skilled; and in plant *B* 17% of the workers referred to these aspects of their jobs.

Thus, about 30% of the workers in the small firms find the activity of work the most rewarding of all aspects of their work. In the large firms very few workers appear to receive such rewards; but this does not mean that work activity is a source of deprivation for the *large majority* of workers. Even in the mass production system only 17% of the workers stated that the task itself was the most disliked aspect of work. We can only conclude that the workers in the large plants are relatively *indifferent* – that is, neutral – in their evaluation of the importance of task rewards.

(ii) Social Rewards from Peer Relationships

In chapter 2, it was concluded that size of organization in its association with bureaucratization was inversely related to the *opportunities* for and the *frequency* of shop-floor interaction. The reasons for this were mainly those stemming from the more rigid bureaucratic mode of control in the large plants. However, there is another restriction on shop-floor interaction in the large plants in this sample: namely, the piecework system. Quite simply, if earnings depend on the quantity of output, then time spent talking involves a loss of earnings. However, I think it would be a mistake to see this kind of restriction *solely* as a direct result of the system itself. By *choosing* to work – that is, by staying – in a piecework system and accepting its controls the workers in the large plants had made a decision to sacrifice shop-floor interaction in their pursuit of high earnings. That is to say, it was their *economistic* orientation and *acceptance* of the piecework system that led to their restricted interaction.

The level of experienced rewards from association with peers at work can be assessed by looking to the percentage of workers in each group who mentioned these on-the-job social relationships in response to the question: "What do you like best about working at your present firm?". Again, the results show wide differences by size of organization. On the one hand, 41% of the semi-skilled and 44% of the skilled workers in the small firms reported that the social relationships with work mates were what they "liked best"; on the other hand, in large plant *A* 20% of the semi-skilled and 8% of the skilled, and in plant *B* 8% of the workers, mentioned this aspect of their work situation.

However, as with those aspects of work concerned with the task, the low level of rewards from peer relationships in the large plants does not mean that these workers are conscious of any deprivation as a result of the low levels of interaction. When asked what they disliked most about working at their firm nobody in the large plants (or the small firms) mentioned an unfriendly shop atmosphere or few opportunities for contact with peers. Again the workers in the large plants seem to be indifferent to this non-economic feature of their work situation. But this does not mean that peer relationships are characterized by *extreme* affective neutrality; evidence suggests that super-ficial and casual relationships exist on the shop floor of the large plants. The respondents were asked: "What would you say about the atmosphere in your shop in terms of friendliness — would you say it was very friendly, quite friendly, not too friendly, or very unfriendly?". The results of this question are shown below in Table 8.7.

Table 8.7.   Workers' Evaluations of Shop-floor 'Friendliness' by Size of Organization and Skill Level

	Small firms: Unit and small-batch technology		Large plant *A*: Unit and small-batch technology		Large plant *B*: Mass production technology
	Semi-skilled	Skilled	Semi-skilled	Skilled	Semi-skilled
Very friendly	50%	72%	30%	15%	9%
Quite friendly	41%	28%	65%	50%	78%
Not too friendly	9%	0%	5%	35%	13%
Very unfriendly	0%	0%	0%	0%	0%
Total %	100%	100%	100%	100%	100%
N	22	25	20	26	23

Although workers in the large plants report a less friendly atmosphere than the workers in the small firms only a minority suggested that their shop was unfriendly. As we would expect, the largest single response in the small firms was 'very friendly'; whereas, the predominant response in the large plants was 'quite friendly'. Thus, for the most part, the workers in the large organizations do not view peer relationships as an important source of reward, but neither do they view the restricted interaction as a source of deprivation.

(iii) Social Rewards from Authority Relationships

We saw earlier that there are very large differences between the large and small organizations in the levels of vertical interaction they permit. Also it was pointed out that the more frequent interaction in the small firms was characterized to some degree by norms of particularism and diffuseness. On the other hand, in the large plants the interaction that did occur was seen to be based exclusively on norms of universalism and was restricted to the specific instrumental activities of the enterprise as a system of production. Thus, it was hypothesized that workers in the small firms may receive 'social' rewards from this interaction and that, in some cases, this might take the form of 'status enhancement'. With such low levels it was unlikely that any such rewards would be experienced; rather, it was hypothesized that the extremely impersonal nature of the relationships would be a source of dissatisfaction and deprivation.

In response to the question: "What do you like best about working at your firm?" 22% of the skilled and 19% of the semi-skilled in the small firms mentioned the friendly worker-management relationships. This was not mentioned as a source of reward by any worker in the large plants. When asked what they disliked most about their organization 20% of the semi-skilled and 27% of the skilled workers in plant A and 9% of the workers in plant B mentioned the unfriendly nature of the authority relationships:

> "There's a very poor relationship between men and management — there's nothing personal — you're just a figure at a machine."

> "You're not appreciated here — last week a bloke who had worked here 35 years asked for his cards and they never asked why."

However, these feelings of deprivation are not very widespread in large plants. Further evidence will show that the evaluation of authority relationships is characterized by extreme affective neutrality. Moreover, there appears to be *no* direct association between the structure of *potential* rewards and *experienced* rewards in this case. For example, the lowest levels of management-worker interaction and the highest level of universalism and specificity in the relationships were found in plant B, but here the number of workers who were conscious of deprivation from the impersonality of the system was lower than in the other large plant (A) — 9% as against 20% and 27%.

Table 8.8.   Workers' Evaluation of Their Relationships with Their Foreman by Size of Organization and Skill Level

	Small firms: Unit and small-batch technology		Large plant A: Unit and small-batch technology		Large plant B: Mass production technology
	Semi-skilled	Skilled	Semi-skilled	Skilled	Semi-skilled
'Very well'/ 'Quite well'	100%	100%	95%	92%	87%
'Not so well'/ 'Badly'	0%	0%	5%	8%	13%
Total %	100%	100%	100%	100%	100%
N	22	25	20	26	23

We can further illustrate these differences between the workers in the large and small organizations by looking at their evaluations of authority relationships starting with the level of foreman.

The 'Human Relations' school of industrial sociology has, among other things, stressed the role of supervision in determining employee 'morale'.[1] In short, they have suggested that 'employee-centred' supervision — characterized by a degree of positive affect — is valued by the worker and is, thus, effective in increasing satisfaction and productivity and in decreasing absenteeism and labour turnover. Such theories have not been successful: as I pointed out in part I, the results of such investigations have been notoriously inconsistent. It is hoped that this chapter and more especially chapter 9 will

1 See part I, chapter 3.

Table 8.9.   Reasons for Getting on Well with Foreman by Size of
                   Organization and Skill Level

	Small firms: Unit and small-batch technology		Large plant A: Unit and small-batch technology		Large plant B: Mass production technology
	Semi-skilled	Skilled	Semi-skilled	Skilled	Semi-skilled
Foreman 'leaves us alone'/ 'we never see him'	5%	12%	50%	39%	61%
Foreman is: technically competent	14%	12%	20%	11%	9%
Foreman is: friendly/'known him a long time', etc.	82%	68%	20%	42%	9%
'Don't know'/ Vague	0%	8%	5%	4%	9%
Do *not* get on well with foreman	0%	0%	5%	4%	13%
Total %	101%	100%	100%	100%	101%
N	22	25	20	26	23

be able to clarify some of the difficulties in this area. According to this type of theory one would expect, on the one hand, that (*a*) due to the low levels of interaction and the specificity of the relationships, workers in the large plants would express negative attitudes towards their foreman to a far greater extent than the workers in the small firms, and (*b*) that the impersonal and 'bureaucratic' nature of the authority relationships would be viewed as a source of deprivation. On the other hand, one would expect the small firms to exhibit the features of the 'Human Relations' ideal of worker-supervisor relations.

103

The workers in the sample were all asked how they got on with their foreman and whether this was 'very well', 'quite well', 'not so well', or 'badly'. The rather surprising results, from the point of view of a substantial body of theory, are shown in Table 8.8.

Although some of the workers in the large plants reported that they did not get on well with their foreman the vast majority (95%, 92% and 87%) — like *all* those in the small firms did, in fact, report a satisfactory relationship. The apparent difficulty in the interpretations of these results is partly resolved if we look at the answers to the question: "Why is it that you get on 'very well'/'quite well' with your foreman?" (Table 8.9).

The responses of the workers in the small firms are quite consistent with the type of 'Human Relations' theory referred to above — that is to say, the majority of the answers to the question refer to the 'friendliness' of the foreman. The opposite is true for a large number of workers in the large plants; here the largest single response refers to the lack of interaction as the most important reason for getting on well with the foreman. Thus, far from being a source of deprivation, the low frequency of interaction and the affective neutrality of the supervisor-worker relationship is valued by those in the large plants.

Similar questions[1] were asked about other authority relationships. In the small firms 78% of the semi-skilled and 95% of the skilled workers expressed the view that it was a 'good thing' that they saw their middle management 'regularly'. The most frequently cited reasons for this were that "it creates a friendly atmosphere" (21% semi-skilled and 30% skilled) and that "the manager gives technical assistance" (50% semi-skilled and 55% skilled). The response to the low level of interaction in the large plants was mainly one of indifference. When asked for their opinions on the low levels of interaction 60% of the semi-skilled and 50% of the skilled in plant A, and 81% of the semi-skilled in plant B reported that "it doesn't bother me whether I see him (middle level manager) or not". Furthermore, in plant A 30% of the semi-skilled and 12% of the skilled workers stated that they preferred not to see or talk with managers from this level. Of all three groups in the two large plants only two workers criticized the lack of interaction and expressed the view that the manager ought to come round more often "to show he was taking an interest". The same questions were put with respect to top level management — owners and managing directors in the small firms and plant managers and managing directors in the large plants — and the results are very similar to those above. The workers in the small firms were in favour of frequent interaction and seemed to value this highly. All the semi-skilled

1 See Appendix B for the interview schedule.

and 72% of the skilled men agreed that it was 'a good thing' that they saw their owners 'regularly' and the reasons they gave for this view were almost entirely of an expressive nature. Many workers referred to what can be taken as examples of the particularism and the diffuseness in the relationship: 27% of the semi-skilled and 36% of the skilled in the small firms said that the owners' presence on the shop floor demonstrated that they were "taking an interest in them and their work". This emphasis on the personal treatment was a recurring theme throughout the interviews of the small firm workers. Quite a large proportion (50% of the semi-skilled and 24% of the skilled) in the small firms were quite explicit on this point and stated that frequent interaction created "a friendly and sociable atmosphere". In contrast, most workers in the large plants (plant A: 80% of the semi-skilled and 89% of the skilled; plant B: 91%) stated that it did not matter to them whether they saw their directors or not.

Thus, the workers in the small firms find the personalized authority relationships rewarding. It seems likely that, due to the high levels of vertical interaction, the workers do not distinguish very clearly between peer relationships and authority relationships. *Both* types of interaction are, from the worker's point of view, factors which contribute to the "friendly atmosphere of the shop". Consequently, there is little evidence of 'status enhancement' and/or deference in the work situation of the small firms in question. In the questions on worker-owner interaction very few responses (12%) revealed the presence of a deferential attitude on the part of the workers — but the following statements from workers show that this type of attitude is, in fact, present.

"Yes, it's a good thing that we see the directors regularly, but they are not treated with the proper respect by everyone — there's too much familiarity."

"He's a real gentleman: but we use first names you know."

In the large plants the situation is not quite so straightforward. First, there are two minority responses to the impersonality of the superior-subordinate relationships: one which views this as depriving and one which actually values the *in*frequency of the interaction. However, the most predominant response is — like that towards the other non-economic features of the situation — one of *indifference*. For the majority of workers in the large plants authority relationships are of little affective significance — in either a positive or negative direction.

105

(iv) Economic Rewards

In chapter 7 we saw that there were wide differences between the organizations in the average earnings they provided. Furthermore, in the first section of the present chapter we noted that, on the one hand, the workers in the large plants were oriented to the attainment of high earnings and that, on the other hand, the workers in the small firms were prepared to accept the substantially lower wages of their firms. Therefore, it is no surprise to find that the economic aspects of their employment are the most rewarding and salient for the workers in the large plants. Table 8.10 shows (a) the percentage of workers who stated that economic rewards were what they 'liked best' about working at their firm, (b) the percentage of workers who chose non-economic aspects of the work situation, and (c) those who specifically stated "nothing" or were unable to give an answer — i.e. 'Don't know'.

Table 8.10.   Most Rewarding Aspects of Work Situation by Size of
                Organization and Skill Level

	Small firms: Unit and small-batch technology		Large plant A: Unit and small-batch technology		Large plant B: Mass production technology
	Semi-skilled	Skilled	Semi-skilled	Skilled	Semi-skilled
Economic aspects:					
Wages	0%	4%	25%	46%	56%
Security	0%	0%	5%	12%	8%
Non-economic aspects	100%	88%	35%	19%	8%
'Nothing'/ 'Don't know'	0%	8%	35%	23%	28%
Total %	100%	100%	100%	100%	100%
N*	27	26	20	26	25

N = The number of *responses.*

106

Clearly, then, compared with the small firm employees the workers in the large plants give far greater importance to wages than to other types of reward from work. This, however, does not mean that the workers in the large plants are completely satisfied with their earnings; nor is it legitimate to infer that workers in the small firms are, for the most part, dissatisfied with their lower earnings. The level of satisfaction with wages is shown below in Table 8.11.

Table 8.11.　Level of Satisfaction* with Wages by Size of Organization and Skill Level

	Small firms: Unit and small-batch technology		Large plant A: Unit and small-batch technology		Large plant B: Mass production technology
	Semi-skilled	Skilled	Semi-skilled	Skilled	Semi-skilled
'Completely satisfied'/ 'Quite satisfied'	63%	56%	50%	57%	60%
'A little dissatisfied'/ 'Very dissatisfied'	37%	44%	50%	43%	40%
Total %	100%	100%	100%	100%	100%
N	22	25	20	26	23

* The workers were asked: "How do you feel about your present level of wages? Are you 'completely satisfied'; 'quite satisfied'; 'a little dissatisfied'; 'very dissatisfied'?"

The most important point about these data on the level of satisfaction is the marked *similarity* of the responses from the workers in the large and small organizations. If we accept that satisfaction is a function of both the level of reward and the level of expectation and if, as in this case, the level of satisfaction of two groups receiving different levels of reward is similar, then we must conclude that the levels of expectation with respect to that reward

107

are also different. Thus, all the evidence points to the fact that the workers in the large plants have set their economic wants from work at a higher level than the workers in the small firms.

We have seen that the workers in the small firms are oriented to the attainment of a high level of rewards from non-economic sources — especially task rewards and to a lesser extent rewards from social relationships. This was termed a non-economistic-expressive orientation to work. Consequently, these workers have tended to choose for employment small firms in which they are able to experience these rewards. The low wages provided by these firms are not a barrier to the employment of these workers because their economic wants are set at a relatively low level.

The workers in the large plants are oriented to the attainment of high earnings (economistic-instrumental) and we have seen that they chose their employment with this as their main consideration. However, although a small minority of workers appeared to be deprived by the relatively low level of non-economic rewards in the large plants the large majority were indifferent in their evaluations of these aspects of the work situation. There are two plausible explanations of this type of response and both refer explicitly to the worker's orientation to his employment. Here we are dealing with the way in which a worker evaluates his work situation after having chosen his employment. In the first place, the neutral responses given by the large plant employees may stem from low levels of wants and expectations from work with respect to non-economic rewards. We did, in fact, see that, when asked what were their most important considerations in choosing a job, the large plant workers rarely mentioned non-economic rewards (see Table 8.2). Furthermore, the considerations concerning non-economic factors were *entirely* restricted to task rewards. There is, in fact, more direct evidence to suggest that there are differences in the workers' needs for complex and rewarding work tasks. The respondents were asked: "Do you think that your present job gives you a chance to use your abilities to the full?" and the replies are given in Table 8.12.

For the moment we can exclude the responses of the skilled groups from consideration; the formal job socialization of this type of worker during the apprenticeship usually engenders a high level of expectation with respect to highly rewarding work. Pride in their craft and skills often leads many men to the view that most if not all work is below their capabilities. The most interesting comparisons can be made between the semi-skilled groups. Here a larger proportion of the men in the large plants — that is, those workers with the least complex and varied work — express the view that their tasks are commensurate with their abilities than those in the small firms. It would appear that the desire for complex and demanding work is at a *lower* level

Table 8.12. Percentage of Workers who Consider that Their Job Presents Scope to Use Their Abilities to the Full by Size of Organization and Skill Level

	Small firms: Unit and small-batch technology		Large plant A: Unit and small-batch technology		Large plant B: Mass production technology
	Semi-skilled	Skilled	Semi-skilled	Skilled	Semi-skilled
	59%	68%	80%	58%	74%
N	22	25	20	26	23

among the semi-skilled men in the large plants than those in the small firms. The responses of the semi-skilled workers in the small firms suggest that they possess a very high level of expectation; a larger proportion than the skilled men in these firms expressed the view that their capabilities are more than adequate for the work they have to do.

In a similar way, Morse found that "low need individuals" who were receiving "a low return from the environment" were likely to give neutral responses; that is to say, they were neither satisfied nor dissatisfied.[1] Thus, there is evidence to suggest that the low level of dissatisfaction -- that is, the indifference to non-economic aspects of the work situation − of the workers in the large plants is a consequence of their low level of expectation from these sources of potential reward.

Second, I also suggested in Part I that, given a situation in which the attainment of high earnings *and* a high level of non-economic rewards was not possible in the same organization − i.e. the large plants in question here − those workers who were oriented to the maximization of their earnings and who also valued non-economic rewards would tend to give priority to their economic wants. In such a case we can, I think, say a little more about the way in which such workers will evaluate the non-economic features of their work situation by referring to the concept of *cognitive dissonance*.[2] If an individual must choose between two alternatives, one of which is clearly superior in his view, the decision entails few doubts or conflicts. If, however, the alternatives are more equal in their attractiveness, the choice of one will lead to doubts concerning the appropriateness of the choice. Individuals

1 Morse, *Satisfaction in the White Collar Job*, pp. 37-8.
2 Leon Festinger, *A Theory of Cognitive Dissonance* (Evanston, 1957).

tend to solve this *dissonance* by shifting their evaluations of the alternatives after having made the choice. The worker who in this case has chosen the large, high-wage plant in order to maximize earnings, but who also values non-economic rewards will tend to *deflate* the importance of non-economic rewards. Evidence shows that a large number of workers (about 45%) in the large plants had, in fact, made such a choice; that is, they had sacrificed non-economic rewards in order to secure high earnings. Table 8.13 below shows the percentage of workers who preferred the non-economic rewards of previous jobs and Table 8.14 shows the types of rewards preferred by the large plant workers.

Table 8.13. Percentage of Workers who Preferred Non-economic Aspects of Previous Job(s) by Size of Organization and Skill Level*

	Small firms: Unit and small-batch technology		Large plant A: Unit and small-batch technology		Large plant B: Mass production technology
	Semi-skilled	Skilled	Semi-skilled	Skilled	Semi-skilled
Preferred previous job(s)	23%	20%	45%	31%	48%
Never worked elsewhere/ 'Don't know'	0%	12%	0%	27%	0%
Did *not* prefer previous job(s)	77%	68%	55%	42%	52%
Total %	100%	100%	100%	100%	100%
N	22	25	20	26	23

* "Leaving aside pay, did you prefer any of your previous jobs to the one you have now?"

We can see that about twice as many workers in the large plants preferred their previous employment and, therefore, in choosing their present employment because of its high remuneration, they were prepared to sacrifice non-economic rewards. Thus, it is likely that some workers have tended to deflate the importance of rewarding work in order to resolve the dissonance caused

Table 8.14. Type of Rewards Preferred in Previous Job(s) by Large Plant Workers by Skill Level

	Large plant A: Unit and small-batch technology		Large plant B: Mass production technology
	Semi-skilled	Skilled	Semi-skilled
More rewards in task	44%	31%	62%
More friendly/more scope for social contacts	44%	31%	19%
Friendlier/more helpful management	0%	38%	19%
Better physical conditions	11%	0%	0%
Total %	99%	100%	100%
$N*$	9	13	16

* N = The number of *responses*.

by their choice of employment.

The nature of the data and the research design does not allow an analysis which might attempt to assign weights to these alternative explanations. Moreover, they are not necessarily mutually exclusive; there is likely to be a middle level of expectation with respect to non-economic rewards which, though not as high as that of some workers, may still require devaluation of non-economic rewards to reduce dissonance. However, the most important point to be noted about both these suggested explanations of the neutral responses of the workers in the large organizations is that they both refer to the workers' *prior orientations* to work as these affect the *choice* of employment and the subsequent *evaluation* of that employment.

Thus, we can conclude that, on the one hand, the workers in the large plants are attached to their organizations almost exclusively by the high earnings they receive. On the other hand, the employees in the small firms are attached not only by the low — but acceptable — earnings, but also by the high level of non-economic rewards they receive. Therefore, as was hypothesized in part I, the similarity of the 'quit rates' and the uniformly high 'stability rates' are the result of different, but *equally effective*, modes of attachment in the large and small organizations. There is also direct evidence from the survey to this effect. In the small firms 45% of the semi-skilled and 52% of the skilled men stated that they had thought of leaving their present employment. In large plant *A*, the figures were 30% and 69% for the semi-skilled and skilled men respectively. In plant *B*, 61% of the semi-skilled men said that they had thought of leaving. Before we examine the workers' reasons for staying in their jobs it must be stressed that very few — with the possible exception of the skilled men in plant *A* — had thought seriously of leaving. When asked if they had approached another employer for a job only 14% of the semi-skilled and 8% of the skilled in the small firms; none of the semi-skilled and 27% of the skilled in plant *A*; and only 4% of the semi-skilled men in plant *B* replied that they had. The reasons given by the workers who had thought of leaving, for staying in their present jobs, clearly illustrate the different ways in which the men in the large and small organizations are attached to their employment. In the small firms 15% of the workers referred to the economic rewards of their job whereas 83% stressed non-economic aspects. In the large plants the proportions are more or less reversed. In plant *A* 72% said that the high wages kept them in their present jobs against 8% who mentioned non-economic rewards. In plant *B* 95% referred to economic rewards.

In this chapter we have seen that there are significantly wide variations in the wants and expectations of the workers in this sample. On the one hand, the workers who had selected the small, low-wage firms had done so in order to attain the high level of non-economic rewards provided by these organizations. From the workers' point of view the most important non-economic requirement was for complex and varied work tasks. A significant minority (about 20%) were attracted to the small firms, *in the first place,* by the friendly social — both peer and authority — relationships. On the other hand, the workers who had selected the large, high-wage plants were oriented to the attainment of high earnings; they were more narrowly economistic in their behaviour. Thus, we saw that there was a high level of *congruence* between wants and expectations and rewards in *both* types of organization and in this way we can explain the similarity of the 'quit rates' and the high 'stability rates' in both the large and small organizations.[1]

---

1 See chapter 1.

9 Involvement and Absenteeism

We have seen that previous work in the field has suggested that the rate of absenteeism is (*a*) inversely related to the level of satisfaction with non-economic features of the work situation, and (*b*) directly related to the level of impersonal controls in an organization. In part I several criticisms were directed at these statements. First, both the above propositions were criticized for the neglect of economic factors. By, rather surprisingly, sub-ordinating the essential economic nature of work to a secondary role — or in some cases neglecting this aspect altogether — these approaches to the problem are to some extent sociologically meaningless. Dissatisfaction or deprivation may mean that a worker is reluctant to attend work, but this is unlikely to be his main consideration. To a large extent absence will be governed by the degree to which the loss of earnings can be afforded. Similarly, a level of identification is not essential to the worker's attachment to his firm; rather, this is an economic link and is basically devoid of 'moral' elements. Second, it was pointed out that whilst deprivation may contribute to absenteeism (within the limits allowed by the worker's economic wants) a high level of rewards in *industrial work* does not necessarily lead to low absence due to the rapidly diminishing marginal utility of such rewards. Thus, it was argued that a clearer understanding of absence behaviour could be obtained if this was viewed in relation to different types of worker *involvement* and referred to as an indicator of the 'effectiveness' of different kinds of control structure.

Worker Involvement in the Large Plants

In the control of the labour force, the managers of the large plants of this study have been seen to rely on *impersonal* regulations and on remuneration. Such rules and regulations cover all aspects of the link between the employee and his organization. For example, the clock card and its number are symbolic of this depersonalized relationship. Apart from major procedural rules designed to deal with discipline (e.g. absence rules) and the work process (e.g. the rules governing job allocation, etc.) there exists a host of minor regulations. Both large plants published a pamphlet of such rules which were a combination of 'punitive' and safety regulations. No such *formalized* rules were used in any of the small plants. I do not wish to show, as Indik attempted to do, that these rules are viewed with 'repugnance' and are a source of deprivation for the majority of workers in the large plants.[1] Indeed,

---

1 It is significant to note that this hypothesis is not supported by Indik's

evidence suggests that although a minority of workers perceive the rules as deprivative most workers accept them as legitimate and useful. The workers were asked: "Now there are rules and regulations at most firms, but do you think that there are too many rules at your firm?" "Why do you say this?" In the small firms 5% of the semi-skilled and none of the skilled workers thought that there were too many rules in their firms. A larger percentage of large plant workers gave this response, but the percentage was still relatively small — 25% of the semi-skilled and 8% of the skilled in plant A, and 4% in plant B.

When the respondents were asked to explain their response the major reply from those in the small firms was that they could not think of any rules in their organizations (77% of the semi-skilled and 84% of the skilled men). In large plant A, 40% of the semi-skilled and 49% of the skilled and in plant B 69% of the men expressed the view that all the rules were fair and were there for a purpose.

Rather, I wish to emphasize that the use of impersonal procedural rules inhibits the *identification* of the worker with his enterprise. In a large organization of the type we have discussed the management and the goals of the organization seem remote. We saw in the last chapter that, although a minority of the workers in the large plants were dissatisfied or felt deprived by the impersonality of the system (see chapter 8), the majority of the men were neutral and indifferent in their evaluations of their authority relationships. Thus, identification and a relatively high level of positive affect do not characterize the relationship between the organization and the employee in these plants. Management must, therefore, rely on *remunerative* controls. Some type of 'payment-by-results' system was used in both large plants and because of the workers' highly instrumental orentiations to work they responded to this type of control.[1] In the last chapter we saw that the level of remuneration was effective in keeping the men in their employment. Thus, management's reliance on remunerative power and the workers' highly

---

data. See Indik, 'Organization Size and Member Participation', p. 347.

1 It is interesting to note that in one of the small firms where a time bonus scheme was in operation the times allowed for jobs had not been changed since 1938 (though, of course, the rate for job had increased). I would take this to indicate a low level of pressure from the shop floor in economic matters. The differences between the two types of organization in the sensitivity of their workers to the 'effort bargain' can be further illustrated by the nature of the workers' grievances. In plant A 60% of the semi-skilled and 73% of the skilled and in plant B 52% of the men had been involved, at some time, in a piecework or wage rate grievance; whereas, the incidence of wage rate grievances in the small firms was 9% among the semi-skilled and 16% among the skilled.

instrumental orientation to work resulted in *calculative* involvement. In other words, the work situation was defined as a means to extrinsic ends — and, as we have seen, little affect (in either a positive or negative direction) is injected into the work situation. The behaviour of these workers is not based on either obligations to employers or a sense of solidarity with fellow workers, but rather on an individualistic pursuit of high earnings. This type of behaviour is revealed in many ways and especially so in plant *B*. The situation in plant *B* was of the type that has often been associated with output restriction[1] and overt management-worker conflict. That is, the shop comprised 90% relatively low skill semi-skilled workers who performed their tasks on individual lathes in a piecework system. Many workers in this plant expressed the view that the constant readjustment of times and rates for the jobs were, in fact, disguised methods of rate-cutting. Although the employer-employee relationship was, *basically,* characterized by low affect some workers were conscious of exploitation and 'unfair' management practices; 22% of the workers in plant *B* responded in such a way to the question which asked them what they disliked most about their plant. Consequently many of the men stressed that unions were necessary in the day-to-day economic bargaining that took place in the plant as management could not be trusted to keep agreements.[2] However, despite all these factors, there was no group restriction of output in either of the large plants. The chief shop stewards, management and the workers themselves all claimed that the men worked as autonomous individuals and for the most part worked to maximize their earnings.[3] In fact, there is evidence to suggest that there was competition between workers for 'easy' jobs on which high piecework earnings could be made. Also some workers complained that job cards — that is, the card on which a record of the work and the time taken to complete it was made — were taken home (illegally) by workers if the job was an 'easy' one in order that it could not be completed by the night shift or allocated to another worker.[4] In a similar

---

1 See, for example, D. Hickson, 'Motives of Workpeople who Restrict their Output', *Occupational Psychology*, vol. 35 (1961).

2 The workers in the large unionized firms were asked: "Do you think that your interests would be looked after as well if there was no union here and everything was looked after by management?" "Why do you say this?" In plant *A* 85% of the semi-skilled and 81% of the skilled and in plant *B* 95% of the semi-skilled men replied that unions were essential to protect their economic interests.

3 Some older workers in the large plants said that control of output on a group or individual basis had been quite prevalent in some shops about ten years ago, but stressed that this had now changed.

4 It is tempting to compare this type of behaviour with Mayo's statement about workers' responses to financial incentive schemes quoted on p. 43, note 4.

way this narrowly calculative involvement tended to inhibit strike action. The chief shop steward in plant B complained that it was almost impossible to get the men to strike as a loss of immediate earnings was foremost in their minds.[1] An ex-miner from South Yorkshire, who was used to the solidarity of his former workmates, but now working in plant B, is perhaps best qualified to speak on this matter:

> "It's nothing like the pits here — they stick together there. We had a one day token strike a few months ago and all they (plant B workers) could do was moan about how much they had lost. If one bloke is making a good bonus he doesn't care if the next man to him is flogging himself to death for nothing. There's lots of 'fuck you Jack, I'm alright' at this firm."

Later in this chapter I will point to ways in which the calculative involvement described here affects absenteeism.

Findings such as those presented above do not appear to fit well with the generalizations of much writing on the 'size-effect'. It is generally assumed in much industrial sociology that employment in large, bureaucratized plants leads the workers, as a collectivity, to take on a solidaristic anti-management outlook. Furthermore, the suggestion is often made — on the basis of a certain amount of evidence — that such attitudes form the basis for political beliefs and behaviour of a left-wing and anti-capitalist kind. I would not wish to question the assertion that the social structure of large-scale industrial plants is favourable to the development and/or reinforcement of such attitudes. Rather, I think it would be a mistake to see the kind of response referred to above as a *direct* and *automatic* consequence of such intra-organizational factors. Large scale will tend to inhibit the identification of the worker with

---

1 Plant B has had one major strike — lasting one week — in the last five years and plant A has been strike-free for many years. I do not wish to suggest that extreme calculative involvement eliminates strikes. In fact, this type of involvement is *unstable*: stability is only achieved if the workers' economic expectations are met. If these are revised in an upward direction then wage disputes are likely to occur. However, the workers in these large plants are among the most highly paid in the area which is characterized by the low wages of the depressed textile industry. The stability of the industrial relations at these two plants suggests that the workers are taking their own area as the reference point for their own expectations with respect to wages. It is significant that the strike in plant B referred to above involved the men's refusal to do work, which had been transferred to Bradford from a Midlands branch of the same group of companies, at a lower rate than was paid in the Midlands plant.

the plant; but antagonism and conflict do not necessarily follow from a lack of such identification. The workers may be identified to all but a few *narrowly* economic aspects of their situation. It is my contention that the individualistic and calculative attitudes of many of the large-plant workers of this study are a consequence of their defining their work activity in an *economistic* way. Moreover, in the following chapter I will attempt to demonstrate that such definitions can be explained at least in part by reference to the *outplant* influences to which many of the workers have been subjected.[1]

Worker Involvement in the Small Firms

Managerial control in the small firms relies not only on the control of remuneration, but also on a significant level of *identive* power. This is made possible by the workers' calculative/*moral* involvement.[2] Moral involvement in the organization may stem from two sources: (*a*) *direct* identification with the goals of the management and the organization, and (*b*) identification with the peer group which may, under certain conditions, become an *indirect* source of commitment to the wider organization. In both cases this type of involvement is characterized by a high level of positive affect.

(*a*) In the last chapter we saw that the majority of workers in the small firms value the close 'personalized' authority relationships of their organizations. All of the semi-skilled and 72% of the skilled men agreed that 'it was a good thing' that they saw their owner 'regularly'. One of the most important aspects of this relationship from the worker's point of view is that the owner's presence on the shop floor demonstrated that he was "taking an interest in them and their work" (27% of the semi-skilled and 36% of the skilled). This *acceptance* by the owners of the workers as 'persons' — that is, the particularism of the relationship appears to be an important source of identification. The following illustrative quotes give an indication of the type of attitude

---

1 It is relevant to note that an examination of the evidence reveals that the 'size-leftism' generalization appears to hold only when certain outplant factors — such as community structure — have been controlled. For example, the workers in small-scale plants in French industry are unusually radical and this is almost certainly due to the location of many small plants in traditionally left-wing communities. In the present study, it is significant that the Conservative vote in plant *B* was higher than that usually found in large industrial plants. Although the evidence from this particular investigation is scanty it points to the fact that a disproportionate number of Conservatives had been exposed, *outside* their present employment, to middle-class influences. See Geoffrey K. Ingham, 'Plant Size: Political Attitudes and Behaviour', *Sociological Review*, n.s. vol. 17 (1969).

2 See chapter 3 for a discussion of the terminology.

I am referring to:

> "The owner takes the men into his confidence about their problems — it's not just about the work you know."

> "You can talk to him if you have any problems — he takes an interest in you as a person."

> "I'd rather have a boss who is sociable with the men and who gets to know how a bloke's mind works — it can help with the problems."

Moreover, 19% of the semi-skilled and 22% of the skilled said that these 'personalized' authority relationships were what they liked best about working at their firm. Many workers' statements referred to the rewards to be gained from identifying with the enterprise:

> "It's a good thing that we see the owner regularly — it gives a man an incentive — he works with you and makes you feel interested in the firm."

> "They (the owners) show an interest in the work and make you feel that the work is important."

(b) Second, affective peer group relationships are also a source of moral involvement. Nearly half of the workers (41% of the semi-skilled and 44% of the skilled men) in these firms said that the friendly peer relationships were what they liked *best* about their present employment. Furthermore, of those who had thought of leaving 20% of the semi-skilled and 41% of the skilled workers stayed in their jobs because of their affective ties with workmates. It must, of course, be pointed out that, with respect to the wider organization, work group cohesion may tend towards positive or negative extremes depending on whether or not the work group identifies with the goals of the management[1]

However, we have seen that in this case the work group's orientation to authority is affective in a positive way.

It must be remembered that the calculative/moral involvement of these workers in the small firms is not only a consequence of their working in a

---

A solidary work group whose members do not identify with the organization can form the basis for resistance to managerial control — e.g. by control of output, work to rule, strike action, etc.

system whose structure is conducive to close interpersonal relationships. Some of the workers *accept* these relationships and therefore respond to identive controls because of their prior orientation to work[1] About 20% of these workers stated *explicitly* that their main reason for choosing a small firm for employment was the special nature of these organizations' social relationships. Furthermore, I would suggest that, although such considerations were not of high motivational importance in job choice, the majority of workers were predisposed to the *evaluation* of work-based social relationships in terms of cooperation and consensus rather than antagonism and conflict.

Thus, the majority of workers in the small firms are not merely attached to their enterprises in an economic way, but exhibit some degree of *commitment*. Thus, attendance at work may have a 'moral' as well as economic significance.

We can now assess the relevance of this approach for the problem of absenteeism. The respondents were asked to choose between two different normative orientations towards absence from work:

(A) "A man should not stay away from work in any event, except when it is really necessary as in the case of genuine sickness."

(B) "It's a free society and a man has the right to take a day off work once in a while if he wants to."

The results of this question (Table 9.1) do, indeed, show that attachment — that is, the view that absence for reasons other than illness is unjustified — is at a higher level in the small firms. But what is, perhaps, surprising is the relatively high number of workers in the large plants who also subscribe to this view — about two-thirds of those in the large plants chose alternative (A).

However, there are important differences, between the groups of workers, in the reasons they give for choosing alternative (A) and, further, these differences are consistent with the differences in their respective types of involvement. Of those in the small firms who agreed with the first alternative the most frequently cited reason for this choice involved their *duty* and *responsibility* to the firm (62% of the semi-skilled and 65% of the skilled men). Quite clearly, these are the responses of morally involved workers. We have already seen that a high level of organizational identification exists among this group of workers and the following statements, which were given as reasons for choosing alternative (A), provide further evidence of this.

---

1 Managers in three of the small firms said that they often employed what they called "the type with a chip on his shoulder" or "the communistic (*sic*) type of man", but they all added that they did not stay very long as they "did not seem to fit in with the men". It is also interesting to note that one of the respondents from plant B mentioned that he had worked at small firm C of this study and volunteered the remark that he had left

Table 9.1.   Attitudes to Absence by Size of Organization and Skill Level

	Small firms: Unit and small-batch technology		Large plant A: Unit and small-batch technology		Large plant B: Mass production technology
	Semi-skilled	Skilled	Semi-skilled	Skilled	Semi-skilled
(A) A man should not stay away from work except in the case of genuine sickness	86%	80%	70%	62%	61%
(B) It's a free society, a man has the right to take a day off if he wants to	14%	20%	30%	38%	39%
Total %	100%	100%	100%	100%	100%
N	22	25	20	26	23

"(B) is not fair to the employer — he's given you a job and if you have to be off work you should let them know so that they can arrange things in your absence."

"You must do a fair day's work for a fair day's pay — the boss can't get anywhere without his profits."

"If the employer is good enough to give you a job you owe him some loyalty."

"I've had half a day off in fourteen years — I don't like to let them down — I like a small firm where you can build up loyalty."

"Time-breaking is a bad habit; if the bosses are getting you work it's your duty to do it."

because the boss was "always breathing down his neck". However, the large majority of workers in this firm *valued* the close authority relationships.

A further 10% of the semi-skilled and 19% of the skilled men in the small firms said that absence would disrupt their workmates' schedules and therefore chose the first alternative. These responses illustrate the 'social commitment' of the worker in the small firm – i.e. his sensitivity to the pressures of the work group which, allied to the high level of identification with the organization, leads to high attachment.

In contrast, in the large plants the largest single group of reasons for choosing alternative (A) concerns the fact that absence involves a loss of earnings: in plant A 42% of the skilled and 50% of the semi-skilled, and in plant B 50% of the semi-skilled men stated that they could not *afford* to be off work:

> "A man cannot afford to be off work – sickness is a luxury the working man cannot afford."

The consequences of calculative/*moral* and *calculative* involvement for rates of absenteeism can be further illustrated by looking at the graphs of weekly rates of absence over the year 1965. These absence graphs were compiled from the data from those organizations that closed down for annual holidays (plant B and firms C and G) in order to show the effects of the need for high earnings, before Christmas and the summer holidays, on the weekly absence rates. Figure 5 (plant B) shows quite clearly that *both* short uncertified absences and longer certified absences – that is, 'sickness' fall sharply before the summer holidays and the Christmas break. It would appear that high economic wants are effective in reducing absenteeism: the average weekly rate of absence in plant B is 7.6% but this falls to 3% in the three weeks before each of these holidays.[1] It is likely that absence due to sickness is at what might be called an 'unavoidable minimum' at these times. The absence graph of the two small firms (Figure 6) that closed down for the summer holidays show no such pattern. In those firms absence is randomly distributed throughout the year and this suggests that the absence that does occur is due to 'genuine sickness'.

However, all this is not to say that, given an economistic orientation to work, remunerative controls alone (that is, a control system without a

---

1 This method of looking at rates of absence as an indicator of the strength of workers' economic needs has been almost entirely neglected due to the overemphasis on the moral integration of industrial enterprises. Moreover, if we accept that the basic mode of involvement of industrial workers is calculative, then this approach is likely to be very fruitful. The fluctuations is absence noted in plant B could *not* have been explained by reference only to the level of worker deprivation and identification.

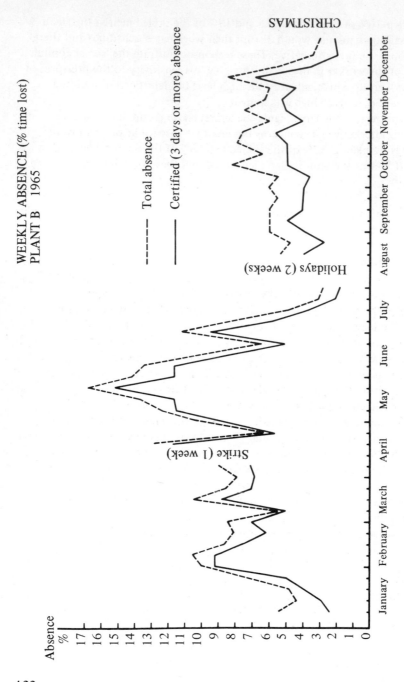

Figure 5. Weekly Absence, in Percentage of Time Lost, of Plant B, 1965

122

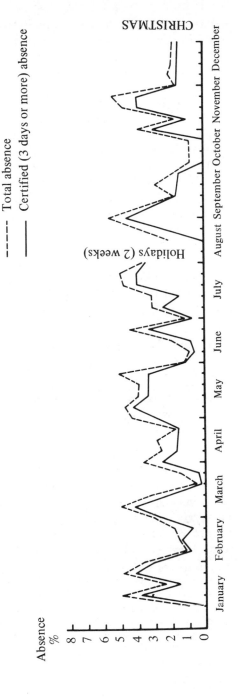

Figure 6. Weekly Absence, in Percentage of Time Lost, of Firms C and G, 1965

123

significant degree of identive power) are *ineffective*. When one refers to, say, the miners' 15% absenteeism the rates of between 4% and 7% for the large plants of this study are quite low. *It is not so much that the rates of absence in the large plants are high, but that the rates of the small plants are very low.*

Further absence data (Table 9.2) suggest, as do the graphs, that moral involvement tends to lead to a reduction in absence due to sickness. The fact that short (less than three days) absences comprise a far larger proportion of the total absences in the small firms than the large plants may be interpreted as being due to the small firm workers' unwillingness to extend sickness absences. The definition of how sick a person must be in order to take a day off work will vary with orientation to work and organizational involvement. That is to say, the committed workers of the small firms are more likely to go to work when sick than the calculatively involved workers who may only do this when economic needs are at a high level.[1]

Table 9.2. Short Absences (Three Days or Less) as a Percentage of the Total Time Lost Through Absence by Size of Organization

	A	B	C	D	E	F	G	H
Size	5,000	3,000	63	26	24	16	12	9
Absence*	14%	17%	26%	26%	31%	61%	41%	31%

* In the calculation of the absence figures the rates for the skilled and semi-skilled workers were combined in each organization.

Thus, we can conclude by stating that *the rate of absence varies inversely with the levels of moral involvement and identive power in an organization.* Therefore, as moral involvement and identive power are inversely related to size of organization (given a prior orientation to work by which workers accept identive control), the rate of absence is directly related to size of organization. However, an important additional statement must be made. In a

1 See the remarks of Charles Kadushin: ". . .absenteeism means loss of pay for wage earners, something to be anxious about. It may also be true, however, that working class persons are less motivated to go to work when barriers such as illness are present. The interaction between attitudes to work, anxiety about supporting one's family and barriers to performing one's job remains to be studied." Charles Kadushin, 'Social Class and the Experience of Ill Health', in R. Bendix and S. M. Lipset, *Class, Status and Power* (2nd edn) (London, 1966), pp. 406-12.

situation where moral involvement and identive controls are not present *absenteeism varies inversely with the level of workers' economic needs.* It is unlikely, however, that in a situation of full employment remunerative controls *alone* can be as effective as identive power and the commitment of the morally involved worker in reducing absenteeism.

10 Some Sources of Variation in Orientation to Work

In this attempt to trace the sources of differences in orientation to work to out-plant factors I will be only able to offer suggestions for an explanation of this problem. As I said in part I, this chapter will have to be looked on as exploratory — but I hope it will prove to be exploration in the right direction. There are two main reasons why this chapter is incomplete. First, limited time made it difficult to follow up every implication of the research. Second, and more to the point, is that in the years since the first ideas about the

Table 10.1. Economism-instrumentalism Measure

Item	0	1	2
Nature of priorities in job choice:* Relative emphasis given to economic and non-economic rewards	Only non-economic rewards mentioned	Both economic and non-economic rewards mentioned	Only economic rewards mentioned
Sensitivity to increases in earnings:+ Increase in earnings required for respondent to leave present employment	Would be prepared to leave for over £4/Would not be prepared to leave for any amount	Would be prepared to leave for between 30s. and £3	Would be prepared to leave for £1 or less
Type of rewards valued:‡ Relative emphasis given to economic and non-economic rewards	Only non-economic rewards mentioned	Both economic and non-economic rewards mentioned. "Nothing" found rewarding. "Don't know"§	Only economic rewards mentioned.

research were formulated I have come to understand some problems more clearly. The problems involved in locating the sources of variations in orientation were only partly understood when the work started. Consequently, certain data that would have been important to this analysis were not collected.

The main problem is to account for the wide differences in *economism* and *instrumentalism* between the workers in the large and small organizations. On the one hand, we have seen that one group of workers have tended to define 'adequate' pay at a relatively low level in order to gain some of the non-economic rewards to be found in the small firms. On the other hand, other workers have chosen to pursue high earnings almost exclusively. This contrast is most marked between the semi-skilled workers in the sample.

Notes to Table 10.1

* "Suppose you were looking for a job, what would be your most important consideration?"

\+ "Would you be prepared to leave your present firm for another if by doing exactly the same kind of job and working the same number of hours in this other firm you could earn 10s. per week more?"

If the respondent answered 'no' the offer was increased to 15s. and so on until over £4 was offered.

‡ "What do you like best about working at your present firm?"

§ In many ways this category and classification is unsatisfactory. The score of 1 for those who mention both economic and non-economic rewards is quite straightforward. The problem lies with the classification of the "Nothing" and "Don't know" responses and it must be noted that the methods used to resolve this difficulty are somewhat arbitrary. A response of "Nothing" to the question: "What do you like best about working at your present firm?" can be taken to signify negative affect or affective neutrality in the evaluation of the work situation. In the event of the latter being the case this would be the response of an instrumentally oriented worker. However, in order not to 'overscore' the instrumentally oriented workers this response has been assigned a score of 1. The score of 1 for the "Don't know" response is a little more arbitrary and this strategy was followed merely to *minimize* the distortion that might occur in the scores if these responses were given either 2 or 0. Moreover, as only 20 out of a total of 124 responses to this question fell into either of these categories it is safe to assume only minimal distortion in the scores.

Skilled workers can usually combine fairly complex work and high pay; but high pay in semi-skilled work usually involves monotonous or physically arduous activity. To be sure, the skilled workers in this study exhibit differences in their levels of economism and instrumentalism but their work situations are more similar than those of the respective semi-skilled groups. In other words the alternatives involved in their choice of employment did not form the sharp dilemma faced by the semi-skilled men. Of these semi-skilled workers one group had chosen to work in a monotonous mass production technology for an average gross weekly wage of £19. 10s. 0d.; whereas, another group were prepared to work for between £3 and £6 per week less in firms which provided a 'friendly' atmosphere and relatively interesting work.

In order to make a systematic attempt to trace the sources of these variations in orientation to work it was decided to construct a 'measure' of economism and instrumentalism from the respondents' answers to certain questions on the interview schedule. It must be pointed out that this is a *post factum* construct and suffers a certain crudeness as a consequence. However, despite this difficulty it is able to differentiate the workers in the sample in a meaningful way. Two criteria were used in the construction of the measure. First, it was recognized that it should attempt to reflect the workers' 'money-mindedness' (economism) and their differences with respect to the value placed on non-economic rewards (instrumentalism). Second, the choice of items to be included in the measure should be from questions that were put to all respondents. Table 10.1 below shows the items that were included in the measure, the scores given to them, and the questions from which they derive.[1]

Thus the most economistic and instrumental workers would score 6. These men have reported that they give importance only to economic rewards in considerations about job choice: they have said that they would be prepared to leave their present employment for £1 or less; and have stated that they find economic aspects of their work most rewarding. On the other hand, the most non-economistic and expressive workers would score 0. These would be the workers who give priority to non-economic rewards in job choice; who would need to be offered over £4 to leave their present firm or would not leave at all; and who view the non-economic aspects of their work situation as most rewarding. The distribution of the scores by skill level and size of organization is shown below in Table 10.2.

---

1 See for comparison a similar measure of 'instrumentalism' used by Gold-thorpe and his associates in the Luton study. Goldthorpe *et al.*, *The Affluent Worker: Industrial Attitudes and Behaviour.*

Table 10.2. Economism-instrumentalism Scores by Size of Organization and Workers' Skill Level

		High		Intermediate			Low	
		6	5	4	3	2	1	0
Small firms	Semi-skilled	0	0	0	2	8	10	2
	Skilled	0	0	2	0	9	9	5
			0		21			26
Large plant A	Semi-skilled	0	6	8	2	4	0	0
	Skilled	5	7	6	5	2	0	1
			18		27			1
Large plant B	Semi-skilled	7	9	5	2	0	0	0
			16		7			0
N		12	22	21	11	23	19	8
			34		55			27

The distribution of the scores falls into two fairly large clusters at either side of the mid-point of 3: fifty-five men scored 4 or more and fifty 2 or less, with eleven men scoring 3. However, in order to assess how far very high economism and instrumentalism are related to the relevant out-plant factors the scores have been divided into three groups: high or economistic-instrumental orientation (scores 6 and 5); intermediate (scores 4, 3 and 2) and low or non-economistic-expressive orientation (scores 0 and 1). As one would expect from an examination of the data in previous chapters there exists a very marked relationship between economism-instrumentalism and size of organization. *All* the high scores fall in the large plant groups and all, but one, of the low scores in the small firm category. The present problem is, therefore, to attempt to determine how far these variations are best seen *primarily* as a consequence of different work situations or if they can *also* be linked in a meaningful way to the workers' non-work situations and experiences.

This analysis can be conveniently approached in three sections. The first one will deal with the effect of certain life-cycle factors; the second with consequences of geographical and social mobility; and the third with the possible way in which socialization in previous occupations and jobs may build up a worker's definition of his wants and expectations from work.

(i) Life-cycle Factors

In this respect it has been suggested that highly economistic workers may be found to be a disproportionately large extent amongst young married men with dependent children, the argument being that sheer economic exigency will motivate men to attempt to maximize their earnings. Some evidence suggests that this hypothesis is, perhaps, ill-founded.[1] In fact, the data from the present study shows that there is scarcely any relationship between having dependent children and the possession of a highly economistic-instrumental orientation to work. Of the fifty-three workers with dependent children, fifteen (28%) were high scorers against 12 (27%) of the forty-four men without dependent children. On the basis of this limited evidence it must be concluded that, in this instance at least, economic exigencies in the form of having dependent children do not necessarily lead to a highly economistic-instrumental orientation to work.

(ii) Mobility

The main hypothesis in part I, Chapter 4, concerned the influence of those factors which tend to break down the 'traditional' working class life-styles and lead to a higher level of 'consumption-mindedness'. The main structural features of this 'traditional' working class subculture are: close-knit kin networks, stable homogeneous communities in which friends are invariably drawn from the individual's own class, a high level of occupational stability and continuity both in the case of individual careers and between generations. In this situation the worker's reference group will tend to be the same as his membership group; that is to say, the worker draws his norms and values from the group in which he interacts and is accepted as a social equal. This may lead to the placing of strict limits on the worker's level of consumption. In this situation even if a worker were able to step up his acquisition of consumer durables or change his style of life the response of his fellow group members may be ostracism for his attempting to 'get above himself'.[2] In part 1 I mentioned two processes which are concerned with changes in the structure of working class community and family relationships that may, in

---

1 Shepherd and Walker, 'Absence from Work'.
2 See Merton's discussion of reference group theory. R. K. Merton, *Social Theory and Social Structure* (Glencoe, Ill., 1957), p. 270.

turn, lead to a higher level of 'consumption-mindedness' and economism. First, we can examine the 'privatization-consumption-mindedness' hypothesis. *Privatization* is meant to refer to the state of relative isolation from cohesive kin groups and communities that the worker may experience as a result of, say, geographical mobility due to rehousing. The individual may be privatized due to his own mobility or the mobility of other members of the group. In this way the individual and his immediate family are released from the support their membership group had given their normative standards and from the guidance it had given them in their interpretations of the mass media and advertising.[1] The argument is, then, that the privatized worker is more likely to take the mass media as his referent and thus become more 'consumption-minded' and, therefore, more economistic in his orientation to work. This is not to say, however, that these changes necessarily signify a movement to a middle class style of life in all respects.[2] Second, the economism may be due to *direct* middle class influences. A worker may have been downwardly mobile (inter-generationally) and this may result in the retention of certain aspects of middle class life styles that require a preoccupation with securing high wages.[3] Such influences might also stem from the worker's career mobility. As I will show later the most usual case is of the semi-skilled worker who has had experience of non-manual jobs and their work-place relationships. Another important factor in the exposure of the industrial worker to middle class standards is the status superiority of his wife or siblings. Thus, these two basic hypotheses are as follows:

(i)   Geographical mobility ➤ privatization ➤ consumption-
                                                            mindedness/economism
(ii) Middle class influences   consumption-mindedness/economism
      1. Inter-generational mobility
      2. Intra-generational mobility
      3. Wife's status superiority
      4. Sibling's status superiority

However, the problem is more complex than this and it is possible for there to be a greater interdependence of the variables. First, geographical mobility may be the consequence of prior privatization: that is, cohesive kin networks

1 Katz and Lazarsfeld, *Personal Influence*.
2 Lockwood and Goldthorpe, 'Affluence and the British Class Structure'.
3 Wilensky and Edwards, 'The Skidder'.

and communities would tend to inhibit such movement. Thus, proposition
(i) may be:

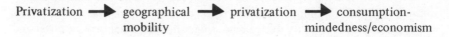

Privatization ➡ geographical ➡ privatization ➡ consumption-
mobility mindedness/economism

Second, middle class influences may in some cases lead to a degree of
privatization as they will tend to preclude the identification of the individual
or the family unit with either the working class or middle class. Such families
may, in fact, subscribe to an inconsistent amalgam of norms from both the
middle and working classes, but may also be rejected socially by typical
members of either class. Thus, proposition (ii) may be:

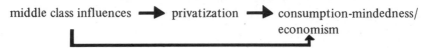

middle class influences ➡ privatization ➡ consumption-mindedness/
economism

Furthermore, all the variables could be associated in some cases.
For example:

middle class ➡ privatization ➡ geographical ➡ consumption-
⬅ mobility mindedness/economism

It would, of course, be desirable to demonstrate all the links between the
variables in the above propositions. However, this will not be possible here
due to insufficient data. Specifically, there is no evidence concerning the
degree of privatization and consumption-mindedness nor the status of the
respondents' wives and siblings. Therefore, I will be able to show only that
mobility and economism-instrumentalism are associated in the way that
one would expect.

Geographical Mobility

Table 10.3 below shows that there is a fairly marked relationship between
high economism-instrumentalism and geographical mobility (movement to
the Bradford/Leeds area within the last ten years).

Eight (24%) of the 34 high scorers had been geographically mobile against
eleven (13%) of the 82 intermediate and low scorers. Moreover, the relationship is much stronger within the semi-skilled group of workers. Here, seven
(32%) of the 22 high scorers had been geographically mobile against seven
(16%) of the 42 intermediate and low scorers. Only two of the 26 skilled
workers in the large plant group had been geographically mobile. This may
be due to the fact that skilled men are more committed to their occupation

Table 10.3. Economism-instrumentalism by Geographical Mobility

	Economism-instrumentalism scores						
	high		intermediate			low	
	6	5	4	3	2	1	0
Mobile	8		7			4	
Non-mobile	26		49			22	
N	34		56			26	

and firm regardless of their level of economic wants and are, therefore, less likely to 'follow the money'.[1]

The next step is to assess how far geographical mobility is associated, *independently* of plant size, with a highly economistic-instrumental orientation to work. Because of the absence of a relationship in this direction among the skilled groups of workers the following analysis will be restricted to the semi-skilled men. With size controlled for, the relationship is much less marked. Seven (32%) of the 22 high scorers against five (24%) of the 21 intermediate[2] scorers in the semi-skilled, large plant groups had been geographically mobile. Thus, with respect to the semi-skilled men in the sample the assumptions regarding geographical mobility receive only a little support. Moreover, as I mentioned earlier there is no possibility of tracing the links between mobility and privatization with the data of this study.

Middle-class Influences

In this particular sample, there appears to be no association between high economism-instrumentalism and middle class influences in the form of downward inter-generational mobility. However, downward intra-generational or career mobility does appear to be associated with this type of orientation; but the relationship holds only among the semi-skilled men. Only one skilled man in plant *A* had ever worked at a job other than engineering and all the skilled men in the small firms had spent the whole of their careers in the same type of job. This occupational stability is obviously due to the skilled worker's

---

1 Cf. Goldthorpe *et al.*, *The Affluent Worker: Industrial Attitudes and Behaviour.*
2 There were no low (1 or 0) scorers among the large plant, semi-skilled workers.

commitment to his occupation and also, perhaps, to the scarcity of skilled labour in the engineering industry in the area.

The workers are considered to have been downwardly mobile in career terms if they have had experience of (i) 'white-collar' jobs such as wages clerk or commercial traveller, (ii) small-scale self-employed occupations – e.g. window cleaner, (iii) supervisory or service employment such as foreman or policeman.[1] Taking the semi-skilled men in the sample as a whole, nine (41%) of the 22 workers who scored high had experienced non-manual employment of some kind compared with 11 (15%) of the 43 intermediate and low scorers. With size controlled the relationship becomes much weaker: within the large plants nine (41%) of the 22 high scorers against seven (33%) of the 21 intermediate scorers had experienced non-manual work situations. However, as it is being argued that it is the influence of middle-class norms that may lead to economistic-instrumental orientations to work there is a strong argument for looking only at downward mobility from previously held jobs that are more unambiguously middle class – that is, 'white-collar' jobs. Table 10.4 shows that there is a very marked relationship between high economism-instrumentalism and experience of 'white-collar' employment among the semi-skilled men.

Table 10.4. Economism-instrumentalism by Experience of 'White Collar' Employment (Semi-skilled Men Only)

	Economism-instrumentalism scores						
	high		intermediate			low	
	6	5	4	3	2	1	0
'White-collar' experience	10		6			0	
No experience	12		25			12	
N	22		31			12	

Ten (45%) of the 22 high scorers had experienced 'white-collar' employment[2] compared with six (14%) of the intermediate and low scorers. Even

1 See Appendix A for a discussion of the occupational classification used in this study.
2 Furthermore, of the nine men in plant B who had experienced 'white-collar' employment five had spent most of their working lives in such jobs.

within the large plant category of semi-skilled workers the association between the two variables is relatively pronounced: ten (45%) of the 22 high scorers against five (23%) of the 21 intermediate scorers had held 'white-collar' jobs at some time in their career. Again, I feel I must point to the limitations of this analysis. Apart from the obvious problems of small numbers and the apparent inability of the hypotheses to deal with the skilled men, there is, with the present data, no way of telling how far the high economism-instrumentalism of these workers is due to (i) middle class influences from their previous 'white-collar' work situations, (ii) outplant association with 'white-collar' families stemming from this job experience, or (iii) privatization due to their somewhat marginal situation *vis-a-vis* both the middle and working classes.

Thus, experiences of geographical mobility and of 'white-collar' employment are most closely associated with high economism-instrumentalism in the semi-skilled group of workers. Moreover, it appears that these two independent variables are to a large degree mutually exclusive — that is to say, there is very little association between geographical mobility and career mobility. Thus, the relationship between high economism-instrumentalism and *both* independent variables is clearly marked (Table 10.5).

Table 10.5. Economism-instrumentalism by Geographical Mobility and/or Experience of 'White Collar' Employment (Semi-skilled Men Only)

| | Economism-instrumentalism scores | | | | | | |
| | high | | intermediate | | | low | |
	6	5	4	3	2	1	0
Geographical mobility and/ or 'white-collar' job experience	15		10			1	
Non-mobile/no 'white-collar' job experience	7		21			11	
N	22		31			12	

Fifteen (68%) of the 22 high scorers compared with eleven (27%) of the 43 intermediate and low scorers had experienced either geographical mobility, 'white-collar' employment, or both. Controlling for size, the relationship is, of course, weaker but still quite clear. Table 10.6. shows that fifteen (68%) of the 22 high scorers against eight (38%) of the 21 intermediate scorers had been mobile socially or geographically.

Table 10.6.　Economism-instrumentalism by Geographical Mobility and/or Experience of 'White Collar' Employment (Semi-skilled Men, Large Plants Only)

	Economism-instrumentalism scores				
	high			intermediate	
	6	5	4	3	2
Geographical mobility and/ or 'white-collar' job experience	15			8	
Non-mobile/no 'white-collar' job experience	7			13	
N	22			21	

With respect to these semi-skilled men it is unlikely that a closer association between the above independent variables and high economism-instrumentalism will be found. I base this assertion on the assumption that high economism-instrumentalism may in some cases be a direct consequence of working in a plant that offers few non-economic rewards. For I would not wish to imply that variations in orientation to work can be accounted for in *every* case and *entirely* by reference to outplant factors. Obviously there are few alternatives to instrumentalism in a plant that offers few intrinsic rewards. Also in some cases 'money-mindedness' — that is, economism — may be engendered and stimulated simply by the receipt of high wages.

Although this analysis has pointed to some ways of explaining the differences in orientation of the semi-skilled workers I have been able to say virtually nothing about the skilled men. Of course, the differences in economism-instrumentalism are less marked than between the semi-skilled groups but there are still differences to be accounted for. Perhaps more information on the 'privatization-consumption-mindedness' hypothesis might have revealed some differences despite the fact that the skilled workers exhibited such a low level of geographical mobility. Two points are relevant here. First, movement of members of the kin group away from the original location of the network may leave the non-mobile members relatively privatized. Second, the geographical mobility we have been considering here is of a fairly long range kind; that is to say, I have not taken note of mobility *within* the Bradford/Leeds area. The fact that this area has a radius of about 10 to 12 miles suggests that it is possible for mobility within this area, and especially that due to slum clearance and rehousing, to lead to privatization.

(iii) Job Socialization

The analysis of the determinants of a high level of 'money-mindedness' does not provide a complete explanation of the problems. As I have stressed, the mere absence of those factors which lead the worker to place a high emphasis on economic rewards does not explain the predisposition to value non-economic rewards highly. The absence of factors leading to 'money-mindedness' may, under certain conditions, be a necessary but not a sufficient condition for a non-economistic-expressive orientation to work. We have also seen that there is evidence to suggest that a fairly large number of workers in the large plants — and especially in plant B — are not oriented to the attainment of a high level of non-economic rewards. This brings us to the second problem: the presence of factors leading to a preoccupation with securing high earnings does not, in itself, explain why some workers have low wants with respect to non-economic rewards in work.

Variations in the value attached to non-economic aspects of industrial work are likely to be the result of prior work experience of different kinds of jobs during which time the worker's priorities concerning non-economic rewards are developed. The process of job changing will involve new experiences and, therefore, redefinitions by the worker of suitable work. Early job choices are less likely to be the result of careful and accurate considerations due to an ignorance of work situations and the range of alternatives. Therefore, expectations with respect to non-economic rewards are likely to develop gradually and to vary with the type of industrial experience. Thus, it is possible, in certain circumstances, for some workers to develop expectations for complex and demanding work and to display a high level of ego-involvement in the work situation. In the absence of

137

pressures to maximize earnings they may, in some situations, be able to meet these expectations. The skilled worker in any type of firm will tend, due to a period of formal socialization in the form of an apprenticeship, to subscribe to a system of norms that emphasize the expressive aspects of work. Semi-skilled workers are, therefore, more likely to exhibit wide variations in the degree to which they seek non-economic rewards from work.

Although it is not possible to assess from the present data in what *types* of work situations — from the point of view of task complexity and social relations, etc. — the semi-skilled workers have been involved it is possible to note some differences between the groups in this category that might be important. In the first place, almost all the men (82%) in the small firms had spent the large part of their working lives in semi-skilled manual work in industry. From this it can, at least, be assumed that these men have had the *opportunity* to build up a knowledge of the availability of non-economic rewards and, further, that they have developed realistic definitions of their wants in this direction. The workers in the large plants exhibit different patterns. In plant *A* 60% and in plant *B* only 56% of the men had spent most of their working lives in semi-skilled industrial work. In plant *B* 38% of the workers had experienced 'white-collar' work and 21% of the sample had, in fact, spent *most* of their working lives in clerical jobs. For two reasons at least it is unlikely that these workers define industrial work as a source of non-economic rewards. First, these men have had little experience of industry and, therefore, have little knowledge of the range of alternatives open to them. Second, manual work is likely to cause 'status anxieties' for these workers after a predominantly 'white-collar' career and as a defence their ego-involvement in work is likely to be at a minimum: that is, their involvement will be characterized by very low affect. Thus, these men are not likely to be especially deprived by the simple tasks and paucity of social relationships in plant *B*. Only those workers who *expect* to receive or are, at least, aware of non-economic rewards in industrial work are likely to be dissatisfied in their absence.[1]

There is, in fact, evidence from the survey to lend a little support — or, more correctly, plausibility — to these assertions. Those semi-skilled workers in plant *B* who have experienced 'white-collar' employment do appear to be, of all the workers, the most *affectively neutral* in their evaluation of non-

---

1 By this line of argument I do not wish to 'define away' all deprivation and dissatisfaction in industrial work. I would like to point out that a level of physical and psychological deprivation will exist beyond which the most highly economistic-instrumental worker will not be prepared to work despite high wages.

economic aspects of the work situation. Table 10.7. shows that this group of ex 'white-collar' men are not as dissatisfied with features of the work situation as the other workers in the plant. Only 44% of the former group were dissatisfied with non-economic aspects of their job compared with 92% of the others.

Table 10.7. Semi-skilled Workers' (Plant B) 'Dislikes' by Experience of 'White Collar' Work

	Experience of 'white-collar' work	No experience
Nothing disliked	55%	7%
Unfair/inefficient management	11%	43%
Unfriendly/ impersonal atmosphere	0%	14%
Boredom/monotony	22%	14%
Poor physical conditions	11%	7%
Other	0%	14%
Total %	99%	99%
N	9	14

These ex 'white-collar' workers display what may be termed 'psychological detachment' from all but the economic aspects of their work. They show neither marked likes or dislikes — that is, they show little affect in either a positive or negative direction.

Inadequate and insufficient data have resulted in what can at best be described as an exploratory and incomplete analysis. However, as implied, I believe that the line of inquiry is justified and that a degree of success has been achieved in tracing some of the sources of the very highly economistic-instrumental orientations of the large plant, semi-skilled workers. The theoretical approach is obviously in need of much refinement and, of course, this would be best attended to by empirical tests of certain links in the argument. For example, a test of the 'privatization-consumption-mindedness' hypothesis is essential. In addition to this much work is needed in the field of job socialization and the possible interplay of personality traits and work experience in the development of non-economic wants from work.

Part III

Conclusions

The main body of research reported in this paper has been concerned with fairly narrow and specific issues in the sociology of industry: namely, the so-called 'size-effect' problem. Indeed, I have only dealt in detail with a small part of this problem. However, I would hope that the work has wider implications. Therefore, my concluding remarks take the form of (i) a brief summary of the themes and findings I have emphasized throughout, and (ii) a discussion of the wider 'size-effect' problem and also of some general issues in the sociology of industry in the light of the present research.

(i)   As I have frequently stressed, the present study diverges from the 'orthodox' explanations of the 'size-effect' in several important ways. First of all, the paper takes as its starting point the frequently uncovered but neglected finding that size of organization and labour turnover do not show as close a positive relationship as many researchers have expected. This hypothesis of a positive size-labour turnover relationship derives from a particular set of theoretical assumptions. The theory on which the hypothesis is based is, by implication, a 'functionalist' one. That is, the industrial organization is viewed as a 'socio-technical system' which has certain 'goals' and relatedly certain 'needs' or 'requirements' which must be met if the goal is to be adequately attained. In the present case, the 'goal' referred to is production and among the 'requirements' is a level of positive motivation to work and produce on the part of the labour force. Thus, from this perspective such diverse patterns of behaviour as striking, absenteeism and quitting the organization are *all* viewed as the same kind of behaviour. These different kinds of action can be viewed as similar insofar as they express workers' discontent which, *regardless of the specific form it takes in behavioural terms, inhibits the attainment of the organization's 'goals'*. Now, I would not wish to criticize this kind of approach merely because it allows the sociologist to group phenomenologically distinct actions (i.e. striking, absence, quitting) into a single cateogry: this would be to deny one of the aims of a discipline which claims to be a generalizing science. Rather, throughout this paper I have suggested that the problems of the 'size-effect' become difficult to solve if one works with the theoretical assumptions outlined above. If one views both absence and labour turnover as forms of 'withdrawal' from work which are symptomatic of the same 'dysfunction'[1] then, it becomes difficult

---

1 Usually, the 'dysfunctional' consequences of the 'socio-technical needs' of the system for division of labour and bureaucracy which are seen as

to explain those situations in which absenteeism and labour turnover vary independently. As I have repeatedly stressed, the similarity of the labour turn-over rates of the large and small firms could not have been explained if the 'functionalist' assumptions referred to above had formed the basis for the analysis. In this particular study the 'goals' of the organization have not been taken as the central focus of interest. Rather, it was found useful to work from the premise that workers' behaviour patterns can be more adequately explained if one refers to their 'goals' and the way in which they attempt to attain them. Furthermore, the assumption of a single 'model' of the industrial worker with fixed 'needs' and 'goals' was also discarded. The main features of this 'image' or 'model' of the industrial worker were outlined in chapter 3. Here it was suggested that most studies of variations in the rate of 'with-drawal' assume that *all* industrial workers are oriented to the attainment of a high level of intrinsic satisfaction from work activity and also satisfying social relationships at work. Thus with this line of argument, labour turnover and absenteeism are seen as responses to work situations in which these 'needs' and 'goals' are not fulfilled and attained. If 'needs' and 'goals' are fixed — that is, form constants in the analysis — then, all variations in labour turnover and absenteeism must be explained in terms of variations in the structure of potential task and social rewards in work. I do not wish to claim that there is anything *intrinsically* unsound about the procedure of positing a 'model' of man in *all* sociological analyses. My objection to this method is similar in kind to the one made against the 'functionalist' framework. That is to say, I believe that the explanatory framework outlined above is *inappropriate* for the present problem. Quite simply, the approach in question is unable to suggest a way of explaining why organizations with widely differing structures of potential rewards can have very similar rates of labour turnover. This problem, which was basic to the present study, can be solved if one looks not only at variations in the structure of potential rewards; but also at *variations* in workers' orientations to work.

The findings of the research concerning the structure of non-economic rewards in organizations of differing size are more or less consistent with those of previous work. In chapter 7 it was shown that, with technology controlled for, (i) the work tasks in the small firms were more varied and allowed for greater autonomy than those in the large plants, and (ii) that

clashing with the workers' 'social' and 'psychological' 'needs'. For a critique of the 'functionalist' approach to the study of industrial organizations and the presentation of an alternative method of analysis similar to the one used in the present study see: David Silverman, 'Formal Organizations or Industrial Sociology: Towards a Social Action Analysis of Organizations', *Sociology*, vol. 2 (1968).

there was a greater opportunity of social interaction on both the horizontal and vertical levels in the small firms. These variations in the level of potential non-economic rewards were looked upon as consequences of the differences in the level of *bureaucratization*. In addition to the analysis of the levels of non-economic rewards, it was also noted that there was a marked size of plant — wage level relationship. To repeat the conclusions to chapter 7, the small firms offered a relatively high level of non-economic rewards and low wages; whereas, the large plants were the source of far higher wages and a low level of potential non-economic rewards. Subsequent data (chapter 8) lent support to the hypothesis that there would be a significant variation between the large and small plant workers in the degree to which they were oriented to the attainment of economic and non-economic rewards. In short, it was shown that the large plant workers were *economistic* and *instrumental* in their orientation to work; that is they were very sensitive to the economic (especially wages) aspects of their employment and less concerned with non-economic factors. On the other hand, the small firm men appeared to be setting their acceptable wage level at a much lower level and, at the same time, demanded a higher level of non-economic rewards (*non-economistic/ expressive* orientation). Therefore, in *both* large and small organizations there was a high level of *congruence* between the workers' wants and expectations (orientations) and the organizational rewards structure. This kind of approach went some considerable way towards explaining why there was no significant difference between the labour turnover rates of the small and large organizations. Similarly in the discussion of the size-absenteeism question, I think a greater understanding can be achieved if recognition is taken of the workers' definition of the situation. In chapter 9 it was suggested that the high level of bureaucratization in the large plants tended to strip the employee's relationship with his organization of all but the narrowly economic elements. In other words, the large plant workers exhibited a low level of *identification* with their firms. On the other hand, the more informal organizations of work and more extensive management-worker interaction in the small firms provided the structural conditions for a relatively high level of *moral* involvement. Many workers in the small firms were seen to define their work roles not merely in terms of the cash nexus; but also as obligations and duties. However, I do not think that a completely adequate understanding of absenteeism can be gained merely by looking at those features of organizational structure that facilitate or inhibit workers' identification. Two other considerations are important. First, given an industrial organization with a low level of bureaucratization, I do not think that workers respond with identification and moral involvement in any automatic way. There is a little evidence to support the hypothesis that a low level of bureaucratization

143

only leads to identification if the workers are prepared to accept, or are at least not hostile to, informal controls and frequent and extensive management-worker interaction. Second, the *meaning* of absence to the workers must not be overlooked. If a worker views work to some extent as a duty and obligation, then, this is likely to lead to high attendance. However, the *calculatively* involved worker for whom such considerations are less compelling is obviously not free from all constraints to attend work regularly. Quite simply, absence means a loss of earnings and evidence in chapter 9 points to the fact that absence rates are inversely related to the labour force's economic wants. Thus, if the employees of a large, high-wage plant are *economistic* in their orientation to work it is unlikely that absence rates will be very high.

As I have frequently stressed, it is not only important to give analytical independence to the workers' definition of the situation. My argument has been that the evaluation and interpretation of the work situation by the participants involved is determined by the objective structure of the situation itself and the wants and expectations the workers *bring* to that situation. Thus, the worker's orientation to work is partly determined by certain out-plant factors. In this connection, a central part of chapter 10 was an attempt to provide evidence for a hypothesis that linked *economism* to the worker's experience of geographical and/or social mobility.

(ii) Although most work has been done with reference to industrial organizations, the 'size-effect' is assumed to be present in all types of organization. If we examine the thesis in its simplest and most general form it is possible to formulate a more widely applicable hypothesis and also to expose some difficulties and misplaced assumptions with regard to the 'size-effect' in industry. The basic thesis is that size is positively associated with bureaucratization and, in turn, that bureaucratization is inversely related to organizational identification and commitment and, therefore, to organizational effectiveness. (Absenteeism and labour turnover rates are relatively adequate indicators of some aspects of effectiveness; if these forms of behaviour rose to a certain level the organization would cease to exist.)

The first point I wish to make[1] concerns the size-bureaucratization relationship. The theory suggests that large-scale organizations create a situation in which (*a*) all or most lower participants are unable to interact directly with one another and thus develop a minimum level of normative consensus, and (*b*) a situation in which the 'visibility'[2] of the elite and the

---

1 The following discussion again relies heavily on the insights provided by Etzioni's work.
2 This concept is taken from Merton's work on reference groups. (R. K.

goals of the organization are insufficient to induce identification with the organization. This hypothesis, by referring to inadequacies in organizational socialization assumes that all major socialization occurs within the organization. This is, of course, not always the case. For example, members of a church who join on a voluntary basis are usually pre-socialized in some basic way in units external to the organization — such as the family. Therefore, we can add a qualification to the effect that in those situations where organizations rely heavily on internal socialization for adequate performance the 'size-effect' will be most pronounced.

Second, the basic hypothesis contains assumptions about the role and importance of organizational identification and primary, informal controls. It is assumed (implicitly) that the 'moral' involvement of the lower participants is *equally* important for effectiveness in all types of organization. However, this is not the case; organizations vary in the degree to which they utilize identive power. In Etzioni's scheme there are three major types of power: coercive, remunerative, and identive. Thus, it is apparent that the 'size-effect' will be most critical in those organizations that rely on identive power and less critical in those that rely on remuneration or coercion for the control of their lower participants. Thus, we can be more precise in the formulation of the 'size-effect' hypothesis and state that: *the greater the extent to which an organization utilizes identive power and relies on the internal socialization and the moral involvement of its lower participants, the more critical for organizational effectiveness will be increases in size.*

These more precise formulations of the problem raise important issues with respect to the 'size-effect' in industry. It has been stressed throughout this study that industrial (utilitarian) organizations do not rely primarily on identive power and moral involvement. This type of compliance structure is present to a significant, though still minor, degree in certain special cases such as the ones we have looked at in this study. Therefore, on theoretical grounds the 'size-effect' in industry should not be very pronounced and, furthermore, I think that it is possible to argue that this is, in fact, the case. First, we have seen that there is no consistent relationship between size and various measures of labour turnover in this and most other studies of the problem. Moreover, certain evidence suggests that, given a highly economistic and instrumental orientation to work, large, high-wage organisations have

---

Merton, *Social Theory and Social Structure* (Glencoe, Ill., 1957), pp. 319-22.) In the context of our discussion 'visibility' refers to the extent to which the norms and role performances of the elite are readily open to observation by the lower participants.

lower levels of absenteeism and labour turnover than industry in general.[1]
Second, only in exceptional cases do absence figures rise very high in 'size-
effect' studies. Often the differences between the rates in organizations of
different size are, though significant, very small. In the present case it is not
that the absence rates in the large plants are very high, but rather that the
rates for the small firms are *very low*. I have suggested that, for the calculatively involved worker, the only barrier to absence is the loss of earnings
involved; whereas, the morally involved worker feels it is his duty to go to
work. Thus, the definition of how sick one has to be to take a day off will
vary with involvement; that is to say, the committed worker will be more
likely to go to work when he is ill.[2] It may be as I have suggested, that it is
not that absenteeism increases with size but rather that calculative/moral
involvement tends to reduce absence due to sickness.[3] Third, evidence
regarding the relationship between another index of 'effectiveness' — namely,
productivity — and organizational size supports this line of argument. There
appears to be even less evidence for the relationship between these two
variables than there is for the size-labour turnover relationship. Moreover,
if it is argued that size inhibits the attainment of an organization's goals then,
in the case of industrial organizations, it might be that productivity per
worker should be taken as a major index of organizational effectiveness.
The study by Marriott[4] of work groups in the motor-car industry is the one
most quoted as evidence for an inverse size-productivity relationship, but it

---

1 Turner, in his study of the British motor-car industry, which characteristically comprises large, high-wage firms, estimates that the average total
absenteeism in the firms of this industry is 5% and continues "...for all
employment the normal percentage of people absent from work because of
sickness or industrial injury for which a National Insurance claim has been
made is also just about 5%. And since this 'compensatable involuntary
absence' is only part of total absenteeism, it seems reasonable to suppose
that the car firms' absence rate is comparatively low" (pp 184-5). With
respect to labour turnover, Turner states that, despite its exceptional
liability to redundancies, the motor-car industry has had much lower rates
of labour turnover than manufacturing generally, or than the neighbouring
engineering and electrical group of industries. See H. A. Turner *et al.*,
Labour Relations in the Motor Industry (London, 1967). If the highly
'instrumental' orientations found by Goldthorpe at Vauxhall are typical
of the motor industry in general, then, reference to this factor would
provide a possible explanation of these low rates.
2 See the remarks of Charles Kadushin, note 1, p. 124.
3 The Acton Society Trust (*Size and Morale,* part II) were surprised to find
that it was absence due to sickness and not uncertified absence that varied
with size.
4 Marriott, 'Size of Working Group and Output'.

must be noted that Argyle has offered an alternative explanation of these results. He states that:

> "It is understandable that group bonus schemes would become ineffective for larger groups; furthermore, in the case of motor car assembly lines the group would depend on the speed of the slowest worker — there is a statistically greater chance that he will be slower in the larger groups. *Despite a general belief among social psychologists in the superiority of small groups, there is no evidence that this is manifested in greater output.*" [1]
>
> emphasis added

Against this evidence is that provided by Revans[2] who shows, with data from collieries and retail sales establishments, that productivity is highest in medium sized units and lowest in the small and large. Herbst's results[3] also show a curvilinear relationship between shop and number of sales per person — but in the opposite direction. That is to say, here productivity was highest in the smallest and largest units and lowest in the medium size ones.

These results are quite consistent with the approach in the study. I have stressed that, despite an expressive component in orientation to work and a relatively high level of moral involvement in some small organizations, the *basic* orientation of industrial workers is economistic and instrumental and that remunerative controls form the basis of managerial power. The notion that the plant is a 'moral community' and that normative consensus is crucial to the functioning of industrial organizations is, in some respects, a legacy of Mayo's somewhat over-zealous interpretation of the Hawthorne experiment and his particular value-laden diagnosis of the ills of industrial society. Most evidence suggests that wage incentives and technological advances are more effective in increasing productivity than identification with the enterprise and/or work group.[4]

In every statement about the consequences of 'situational demands' (due to social, technological, or ecological determinants) for human behaviour lies

---

1 Michael Argyle, *et al.,* 'Supervisory Methods Related to Productivity, Absenteeism, and Labour Turnover', *Human Relations*, vol. 11 (1958).
2 Revans, 'Human Relations, Management and Size'.
3 P. G. Herbst, 'The Measurement of Behaviour Structures by means of Input-Output Data', *Human Relations*, vol. 10 (1957).
4 In a review of the work in this field Argyle (1958) reports that those studies that show a relationship between 'social' factors and productivity have usually noted increases in productivity of about 10% due to the influence of these non-economic factors. Against this he shows that increases of between 20 and 30% have been shown to be a result of wage incentive schemes and improved work methods.

147

an assumption concerning the properties of individuals faced by these demands. Such a set of assumptions is necessary in order to render any explanation meaningful. As I suggested earlier, to neglect the subjective 'meaning' of a situation for the actors involved implies a form of behaviourism. Therefore, if these assumptions are necessary it is desirable that they are *explicitly* formulated at the beginning of any analysis. However, we have even seen that in many cases these assumptions are only implicit in the analysis. Only by looking at the consequences of the social and technical factors can one construct the model of the actors' orientations that form a basis for the analysis. I have argued that, not only are these assumptions often implicit, but also that there is often a tendency in industrial sociology to work with an inaccurate model of the 'industrial worker'. In short, the importance of industrial employees' expressive 'needs' in the work situation has tended to be overemphasized and overgeneralized in many analyses.

Of course, if reference to the social and technological features of organizations furnish an adequate explanation in all cases — in the restricted sense of predictive power — then, the worker's definition of the situation can be relegated to a secondary place in the analysis.[1] In such a case it would merely provide a clearer 'understanding' of the behaviour involved than if this factor was left implicit. However, I have taken this approach a stage further and argued that, in many cases, the worker's definition of the situation (i.e. his orientation to work) must be viewed as a variable and not as a constant. This is an empirical problem: that is, I have argued that workers' orientations can be viewed as constants in an analysis of industrial behaviour only if this can be demonstrated empirically.[2] If, in fact, variations in orientation to work can be shown to exist, then emphasis solely on the socio-technical structure of an organization will always yield inadequate results. In the present case the similarity of the labour turnover rates could not have been explained had the analysis worked with the assumptions of previous studies — that is, that *all* workers possess what I termed a non-economistic/expressive orientation to work. Thus, in a situation where variations in orientation are to be found

---

1 I am referring here to the major independent variables used in the 'Human Relations' studies (work group cohesion and supervisory styles) and by those writers who have recently stressed the importance of production technology for behaviour in the enterprise. See chapter 3.

2 Percy Cohen has recently suggested that in large, complex societies "the different institutional spheres have some degree of autonomy; thus different sectors are free to shape attitudes independently of others; and these attitudes may be carried over by some people from one sector to another". Moreover, he suggests that the sociological study of attitudes is of extreme importance in such situations. See P. S. Cohen, 'Social Attitudes and Sociological Enquiry'.

these must be taken as independent variables. In other words, the present concern in industrial sociology with the 'structure of situations' should be coupled with an emphasis on the range of action alternatives open in each situation.[1]

Furthermore, the emphasis on the meaning injected into the situation by the actors enables the study of industrial behaviour to extend beyond the 'factory gates' in the search for explanatory variables.[2] One of the advantages of using the approach that has been presented in this study is that it allows the empirical delineation of some important functional relationships in industrial society to be made. As Gouldner[3] has pointed out, the levels of interdependence, reciprocity and autonomy in a social system are problematic and need to be established empirically rather than postulated in an *a priori* manner. In this respect there has been a conspicuous absence of studies that deal with the very important functional relationship between the worker's roles of producer and consumer. Clearly, much work is required in this area.

The differences in orientations to work we have noted in this study were found within one broad cultural setting in a single urban area and, thus, it is likely that inter-societal variations are even more pronounced. A recent study by Zurcher is relevant in this respect. It was shown that the particularism of a group of Mexican bank employees resulted in a high level of alienation and dissatisfaction in their work situation which was typified by universalistic norms. Their American counterparts who subscribed to norms

---

1 In a similar way Goldthorpe has recently used this type of argument in criticizing the exponents of the 'logic of industrialism' thesis who have suggested that systems of stratification in different societies are likely to become more similar in response to the exigencies posed by an advanced industrial technology. Against this Goldthorpe has suggested that there has been an "underestimation of the extent to which social order may be shaped through purposive action within the limits of such exigencies". J. H. Goldthorpe, 'Social Stratification in Industrial Society', in Paul Halmos (ed.), *The Development of Industrial Society, Sociological Review,* Monograph no. 8 (1964), pp. 97-122.
2 Clark Kerr and Lloyd H. Fisher have pointed out that, due to the substantial output of Mayo-inspired work and the formation of a 'school' that has had great influence on both academic thought and professional practice, "it is an understandable and common error to identify plant and sociology as though it were the entirety of 'industrial sociology' ". 'Plant Sociology: The Elite and the Aborigines', in Mirra Komarovsky (ed.), *Common Frontiers of the Social Sciences* (Glencoe, Ill., 1954).
3 A. W. Gouldner, 'Reciprocity and Autonomy in Functional Theory', in L. Gross (ed.), *Symposium on Sociological Theory* (New York, 1959), pp. 241-70.

of universalism were markedly less alienated and dissatisfied.[1] Lipset has recently argued that American society and especially the political system is characterized by the norms of universalism, achievement and specificity to a greater extent than other advanced societies such as Great Britain or France.[2] In this connection it is interesting to note that there is some evidence to suggest that the 'size-effect' is less pronounced in American industry. Revans shows that whereas the accident rate increases with size in the British coal industry, the rate in American industry rises to a maximum in mines employing from 100 to 300 and then falls sharply with increases in size.[3] Furthermore, data from industry in general in both societies follow the same patterns as those found in the mines. If I could be allowed a very tentative hypothesis it might be argued that the widespread adherence to norms of universalism and specificity in American society enables the employee to function more effectively in large-scale, bureaucratized organizations. In any event I would suggest that comparative studies may yield important and interesting results.[4]

Despite the reaction against Mayoite industrial sociology a large volume of research still tends to place emphasis on the expressive and not the instrumental aspects of industrial behaviour. The two recent and most frequently cited studies[5] of the 'size-effect' in this research provide examples of this overemphasis of the non-economic in economic life. It is interesting to note in this connection that similar charges have recently been brought against political sociology. Poggi suggests that contemporary political sociology shows "...an inability or unwillingness to focus on specifically political aspects" and than an example of this is the "attempt to explain a voter's choice largely as a function of his expressive need - dispositions, rather than of his cognitive assessment of the electoral alternatives open to him..."[6] Thus, in conclusion, it is hoped that the present type of approach to the study of industrial behaviour – that is to say, the emphasis on the worker's definition of the situation – has been useful in focussing on the essential economic nature of work.

1 L. A. Zurcher, et al., 'Value Orientation, Role Conflict and Alienation from Work: A Cross-Cultural Study', American Sociological Review, vol. 30 (1965).
2 S. M. Lipset, The First New Nation (New York, 1963).
3 Revans, 'Human Relations, Management and Size'.
4 It is unfortunate that there appear to be no extensive studies of the size-absenteeism relationship in American industry.
5 Talacchi, 'Organizational Size, Individual Attitudes and Behaviour'; Indik, 'Organization Size and Member Participation'.
6 G. Poggi, 'A Main Theme of Contemporary Sociological Analysis: Its Achievements and Limitations', British Journal of Sociology, vol. 16 (1965).

Appendixes

A. The Occupational Classification

The following table shows the occupational classification that was used in the analysis of the social mobility data that were discussed in part II, chapter 10. I am indebted for the use of this classification to John H. Goldthorpe who with David Lockwood and others developed the classification for use in their study of the 'Affluent Worker'[1].

Table A.1.   The Occupational Classification

1, 2, 3:	*a, b.*	For non-agricultural (*a*) and agricultural (*b*) respectively: 1, higher, 2, intermediate, 3, lower professional, administrative and managerial grades
		e.g. 1, *a* doctors 1, *b* veterinary surgeons
		         2, *a* works managers 2, *b* estate managers
		         3, *a* clerks 3, *b* stewards

1, 2, 3:	*c.*	Differing grades of self-employed in terms of capital and/or employees
		e.g. 1, *c* large-scale employers
		         2, *c* medium size employers
		         3, *c* small-scale employers (under 10 men)

4:	*a, b.*	For non-agricultural (*a*) and agricultural (*b*) 'intermediate' occupations e.g. 4, *a* policeman, 4, *b* bailiff supervisor
4:	*c.*	For 'intermediate' self-employed – i.e. low capital, no employees e.g. window cleaner
5:		Skilled manual workers (apprenticed or equivalent training) e.g. toolmaker, printer

1   Goldthorpe, *et al.*, *The Affluent Worker: Industrial Attitudes and Behaviour.*

6:		Other skilled manual workers not apprenticed – i.e. 'skilled by habituation'
		e.g. skilled miners, unapprenticed mechanics.

7:		Semi-skilled manual workers
		e.g. car assembly line worker

8:	*a, b.*	For non-agricultural (*a*) and agricultural (*b*) respectively: unskilled manual workers

In chapter 10 'non-manual and self-employed' comprises categories 1, 2, 3 and 4 and the term 'white collar' is reserved for categories 1, 2, 3: *a, b* only.

B. The Interview Schedule

Section A

1. When did you first go to work at .... (present firm)?

2. Since then have you ever left either of your own accord or because of redundancy?
   If YES: When was that?
             Why did you leave?
             When did you come back?
             Why did you come back?

3. Have you worked anywhere except at .... (present firm)?
   If NO: Move to question 5.

4.(*a*) What was the last job you had before going to .... ?
       Name of firm
       Location of firm
       Actual type of job
       Skill level
       Industry

4.(*b*) What were the main jobs you had before that: say those you had for a year or more?

4.(*c*) And how many jobs have you had altogether since you started work including your present one?

4.(*d*) Now you worked at .... before you went to .... (present job). Why did you leave?

4.(*e*) Was there anything special about .... (present firm) that prompted you to go there for a job?

4.(*f*) Leaving aside pay did you like any of your other jobs more than the one you have now?
       If YES: Which ones?
                 Why did you like them more?

5. Have you ever thought recently of leaving your present job at ....?
   Say, within the last year?

If YES: Have you done anything about it?
Why have you thought of leaving?
As you have thought of leaving — what is it then that keeps you at .... ?

6.   Supposing you were looking for a job what would be your most important consideration?
If pay only: Would you look for anything else?
If non-economic considerations only: Would you look for anything other than .... ?

7.   What sort of work does your father do or what was his last job if he is no longer alive or has retired?
Has/had he been in that kind of work for most of his life?
If NO: What were his other main jobs?

Section B

1.   Have you served an apprenticeship?

2.   What exactly is your present job? Could you tell me briefly in your own words just exactly what it is you do?

3.   Have you done any other jobs at .... ?
If NO: Move to question 5.
If YES: What were they?

4.   Do you prefer the job you are doing now to others you have done at .... ?
If YES: Why is that?
If NO: Which of your jobs did you prefer?
Why?

5.   What is it that you most like about working at .... (present firm)?

6.   What is it that you dislike most about working at .... (present firm)?

7.   Do you ever move from your usual machine?
If YES: About how often does this happen?
Is it: About 2 or 3 times a week
About once a week
About once a month
About once every two months

8. Do you ever get breaks between jobs or is there always another ready for you as soon as you have finished one?
   If YES: How often does this happen?

   Would you say: Regularly
   Occasionally
   Rarely

9. Do you think that your present job gives you a chance to use your opportunities to the full?

10. Which of these statements best describes how you feel about your job?
    Completely satisfied
    Quite satisfied
    A little dissatisfied
    Very dissatisfied

Section C

1. And how do you feel about your present level of wages?
   Completely satisfied
   Quite satisfied
   A little dissatisfied
   Very dissatisfied

2. Supposing the situation arose, would you leave your present firm for another where by doing a similar job and working the same number of hours you could earn:
   10s. per week more
   15s. ,, ,, ,,
   £1 ,, ,, ,,
   30s. ,, ,, ,,
   £2 ,, ,, ,,
   £3 ,, ,, ,,
   £4 ,, ,, ,,

3. Do you know of any other firms in engineering industry in the Bradford area where you could earn more than your present wage doing the same kind of job and similar hours?
   If YES: Could you tell me which they are?
   Can you tell me why you don't go to this/one of these firm(s)?

Section D

1. How do you get on with your foreman?

155

Is it: Very well
              Quite well
              Not so well
              Badly

Why is it that you get on .... with your foreman?

2.   Which type of foreman would you prefer to work with?
       (*a*)   One who tries to be friendly and takes a close interest both in his men's work and their lives.
       (*b*)   One who just gives out the work and leaves the men to get on with it, seeing them as little as possible.

3.   Do you ever discuss things other than work with your foreman?
      If YES: How often is this?
                 What do you talk about?

4.   (Where applicable) How often do you see your shop supervisor/department head on the shop floor?
      Is it: Regularly
                Occasionally
                Rarely
                Never

How often is this?

Do you think it is a good thing that you see your shop supervisor/department head regularly/occasionally/rarely/never?

Why do you say that?

Do you ever talk to the shop supervisor/head of department?

If YES: What do you talk about?

If talks about work only: Do you ever talk about things other than work?

5.   How often do you see your works manager on the shop floor?
      Is it: Regularly
                Occasionally
                Rarely
                Never

How often is this?

Do you think it is a good thing that you see your works manager regularly/occasionally/rarely/never?

Why do you say that?

Do you ever talk to the works manager?

If YES: What do you talk about?

If talks about work only: Do you ever talk about things other than work?

6. Do you ever see anyone above works manager on the shop floor?
(e.g. directors/managing directors)
Is it: Regularly
             Occasionally
             Rarely
             Never
How often is this?
Do you think it is a good thing that you see your directors/managing
directors regularly/occasionally/rarely/never?
Why do you say that?
Do you ever talk to the directors?
If YES: What do you talk about?
If talks about work only: Do you ever talk about things other than
                                 work?

7. Generally speaking do you consider management at this firm to be:
          Excellent
          Better than most
          Average
          Below average
          Very poor
Why do you say this?

Section E

1. In your job how often do you talk to your work mates?
Would you say it was:
          A great deal
          Now and then
          Hardly at all
How often is this?
Is it: Only at break time
       Mostly at break time
       At any time at all

2. How many people who you work with would you call close friends?

3. Do you see him/them outside the factory?
Is it: Regularly
       Occasionally
       Rarely
       Never
Where do you see him/them?

4. How well do you know his wife and family/their wives and families?
   Would you say: Very well
                     Quite well
                     Just to say hello
                     Not at all

5. What would you say about the atmosphere at your firm in terms of friendliness?
   Would you say it was: Very friendly
                            Quite friendly
                            Not too friendly
                            Very unfriendly

Section F

1. How about the idea of becoming foreman – would you like this:
           Very much
           Quite a lot
           Not much
           Not at all
   Why do you say this?

2. Have you ever thought seriously of becoming a foreman?
   If YES: Have you done anything about it?
   If YES: What have you done about it?

3. What do you think, then, are the chances of a shop-floor worker becoming a foreman in this firm?
   Would you say they are: Very good
                              Fairly good
                              Not too good
                              Hopeless
   Why do you say this?

4. Have you ever been in business on your own?
   If YES: What was this?
   If NO: Would you like to go into business on your own?
   Would you like this: Very much
                           Quite a lot
                           Not much
                           Not at all
   If you would like to go into business: What do you think are the chances of this happening?
   Would you say they were: Very good
                               Fairly good

> Not too good
> Hopeless

If good: Are you making any preparation for this?

5.   Do you know anyone who has gone into business on their own?
     If YES: Who?

6.   FOR UNIONIZED PLANTS
     How would you like the idea of becoming a shop steward?
     Would you like it: Very much
                            Quite a lot
                            Not much
                            Not at all
     Why do you say this?
     If you would like to become a shop steward: Have you ever stood for
                                                     election?

Section G

1.   Now I'd like to ask you how you feel about absence from work —
     here are two views on absence — which one comes nearer to your own
     view?
     (*a*)   A man should not stay away from work in any event, except
              when it is really necessary as in the case of genuine sickness.
     (*b*)   It's a free society and a man has the right to take a day off
              once in a while if he wants to.
     Why do you say this?

Section H

1.   Are you a member of a trade union?
     If NO: Move to question 8.
     If YES: Which?
     Why did you join?

2.   How often do you go to union branch meetings?
     Would you say you went: Regularly
                              Occasionally
                              Rarely
                              Never
     When did you last go to one?
     If rarely/never: Why is it that you don't go to union branch
                          meetings?

3.   How often do you go to shop meetings?
     Would you say you went: Regularly

Occasionally
Rarely
Never

When did you last go to one?
If rarely/never: Why is it that you don't bother with shop meetings?

4.   How about voting in elections for shop stewards?
Would you say you voted: Regularly
                             Occasionally
                             Rarely
                             Never

5.   And how about voting at union branch meetings?
Would you say you voted: Regularly
                             Occasionally
                             Rarely
                             Never

6.   How often do you talk to your work mates about union affairs?
Would you say: Very often
                  A good deal
                  Now and then
                  Hardly ever

7.   And what about the shop steward: how often do you talk to him about your work and conditions?
Would you say: Very often
                  A good deal
                  Now and then
                  Hardly ever

8.   Were you ever a union member?
If YES: What union was that?
Why did you leave?

9.   Have you any objections to joining a union?
If YES: Why is this?

10.   FOR WEAK/NON-UNION FIRMS
Your firm has little/no union organization – why do you think this is so?

11.   Do you think you would gain anything by having a stronger union here?

Why do you say that?

12. FOR UNIONIZED FIRMS
     Do you think that your interests would be looked after as well if
     there was no union here and everything was looked after by manage-
     ment?
     Why do you say this?

Section I

1. Here are two opposing views about industry generally — I'd like you
    to tell me which one you agree with more:
    (a) Some people say that a firm is like a football side because good
         teamwork means success and this is to everyone's advantage.
    (b) Others say that teamwork is impossible because employers and
         men are really on opposite sides.

2. Is there any job outside engineering that you would like to have?
    If YES: What is it?

3. Let's look at it another way: if you were starting out all over again
    would you choose engineering as a job?
    If YES: Why?
    If NO: What would you choose?
    And why?

Section J

1. Have you ever lodged a complaint or grievance concerned with your
    work?
    If NO: Move to question 2.
    If YES: What was it about?

2. Have you ever thought of lodging a complaint or grievance?
    If YES: What was it about?

Section K

1. Now there are rules and regulations in most firms, but do you think
    that these are too many rules and regulations at ....
    (present firm)?
    Why do you say this?

2. Are there any rules you particularly dislike having to follow:
    If YES: What are they?

F   161

3. Are there any rules which you think management are too strict in enforcing?
   If YES: Which ones?
   Why do you think this is so?

4. Generally speaking do you think that in enforcing the rules management are:
   Very strict
   Quite strict
   Fairly lax
   Very lax

Section L

1. Have you been out of work for any length of time?
   If YES: For how long?

2. How secure do you think your job is at .... (present firm)?
   Would you say it is: Dead safe
                         Fairly safe
                         Rather insecure
                         Very insecure
   What makes you say that?

Section M

Well, now we come to a slightly different kind of question: so far we've been concentrating on your work, but now I'd like to get an idea of your thoughts on some other topics so I can get a more rounded view of how you look at things.

1. Could you tell me how you voted at the last few elections?

2. If no change from 1945 or earliest vote:
   Now you seem pretty attached to the Conservative/Labour/Liberal Party – can you tell me why this is?

3. For each change: Why is it that you .... ?

4. (i)   Some people say that the trade unions have too much power in the country – On the whole would you agree or disagree?
   (ii) Some people say that big businessmen have too much power in the country – On the whole would you agree or disagree?

162

Section N

1. Which social class would you say you belonged to?
    If no response with any variant of middle or working class then:
    If you had to say middle or working class which would you say?

2. What sort of people do you mean when you talk about ....
    (respondent's self-rated class)?

3. What sort of people to you mean when you talk about ....
    (the other class, middle or working as the case may be)?

4. How many social classes would you say there are? Could you name
    them?

Section O

1. Age
    Marital status
    Number of children
    Ages of children

2. Do you own or are you buying your house, or is it rented?

Bibliography

Acton Society Trust, *Size and Morale*, part I (London, 1953).
— —, *Size and Morale*, part II (London, 1957).
Adoratsky, V., *Selected Works of Karl Marx* (New York, n.d.).
Anderson, T.R. and Warkov, S., 'Organizational Size and Functional Complexity: A Study of Administration in Hospitals', *American Sociological Review*, vol. 27 (1961).
Argyle, Michael, 'Supervisory Methods related to Productivity, Absenteeism and Labour Turnover', *Human Relations*, vol. 11 (1958).
Argyris, Chris, *Personality and Organization* (New York, 1957).
— —, 'The Organization: What makes it Healthy?'. *Harvard Business Review*, vol. 36 (1958).
— —, 'Understanding Human Behaviour in Organizations: One Viewpoint', in Mason Haire (ed.), *Modern Organization Theory* (New York, 1959).

Baldamus, W., *Efficiency and Effort* (London, 1959).
Behrend, H., *Absence under Full Employment* (Birmingham, 1951).
Bendix, Reinhard, *Work and Authority in Industry* (New York, 1963).
Blau, Peter N., Heydebrand, W.V. and Stauffer, K.E., 'The Structure of Small Bureaucracies', *American Sociological Review*, vol. 31 (1966).
Blauner, Robert E., 'Work Satisfaction and Industrial Trends in Modern Society', in S.M. Lipset and Walter Galenson (eds.), *Labour and Trade Unionism* (New York, 1960).
— —, *Alienation and Freedom* (Chicago, 1964).
Bott, Elizabeth, *Family and Social Network* (London, 1957).

Campbell, H., 'Group Incentive Payment Schemes', *Occupational Psychology*, vol. 26 (1952).
Caplow, T., 'Organizational Size', *Administrative Science Quarterly*, vol. 1 (1957).
— —, *Principles of Organization* (New York, 1964).
Chinoy, Ely, *Automobile Workers and the American Dream* (New York, 1955).
Cleland, Sherril, *The Influence of Plant Size on Industrial Relations* (Princeton, 1955).
Cohen, P.S., 'Social Attitudes and Sociological Enquiry', *British Journal of Sociology*, vol. 17 (1966).
Cook, P.H., 'Labour Turnover Research', *Journal of the Institute of Personnel Management*, vol. 33 (1951).

Dalton, Melville, 'Worker Response and Social Background', *Journal of Political Economy*, vol. 55 (1947).

– –, 'The Industrial Rate Buster: A Characterization', *Applied An*
vol. 7 (1948).
Dubin, Robert, 'Industrial Workers' Worlds', *Social Problems*, vol.
Durkheim, Emile, *The Division of Labour in Society* (Glencoe, Ill.

Etzioni, Amitai, *A Comparative Analysis of Complex Organizations*
(Glencoe, Ill., 1961).
– –, 'Organizational Control Structure', in James G. March (ed.), *Handbook
of Organizations* (Chicago, 1965), pp. 650-77.

Festinger, Leon, *A Theory of Cognitive Dissonance* (Evanston, 1957).
Friedmann, Georges, *The Anatomy of Work* (London, 1961).

Goffman, Irving, *Asylums* (New York, 1961).
Goldthorpe, John H., 'Orientation to Work and Industrial Behaviour: A
Contribution to an Action Approach in Industrial Sociology', Unpublished
paper, Cambridge (1964).
– –, 'Social Stratification in Industrial Society', in Paul Halmos (ed.),
The Development of Industrial Society, Sociological Review Monograph,
no. 8 (1964), pp. 97-122.
– –, 'Attitudes and Behaviour of Car Assembly Workers: A Deviant Case
and a Theoretical Critique', *British Journal of Sociology*, vol. 17 (1966).
Goldthorpe, John H., Lockwood, David, Bechhofer, Frank, and Platt,
Jennifer, *The Affluent Worker: Industrial Attitudes and Behaviour*
(Cambridge, 1968).
Gouldner, Alvin W., *Patterns of Industrial Bureaucracy* (London, 1955).
– –, 'Metaphysical Pathos and the Theory of Bureaucracy', *American
Political Science Review,* vol. 49 (1955).
– –, 'Reciprocity and Autonomy in Functional Theory', in L. Gross (ed.),
Symposium on Sociological Theory (New York, 1959).
– –, 'Organizational Analysis', in Robert K. Merton, (ed.), *Sociology Today*
(New York, 1959), pp. 400-27.

Haire, Mason, 'Biological Models and Empirical Histories of the Growth of
Organizations', in Mason Haire (ed.), *Modern Organization Theory* (New
York, 1959), pp. 272-306.
Hall, Richard F., Haas, J.E. and Johnson, N.J., 'Organizational Size,
Complexity and Formalization', *American Sociological Review,* vol. 32
(1967).
Hamilton, Richard F., *Affluence and the French Worker in the Fourth
Republic* (Princeton, 1967).
Hewitt, D. and Parfit, J., 'A Note on Working Morale and Size of Group',
Occupational Psychology, vol. 27 (1953).
Hickson, D.J., 'Motives of Workpeople who restrict their Output',
Occupational Psychology, vol. 35 (1961).

Hill, J.M.M and Trist, E.L., 'Changes in Accidents and other Absences with Length of Service', *Human Relations*, vol. 8 (1955).

Hill, J.M.M. and Rice, A.K., 'The Representation of Labour Turnover as a Social Process', *Human Relations*, vol. 3 (1950).

Hinings, C.R., Pugh, D.S., Hickson, D.J. and Turner, C., 'An Approach to the Study of Bureaucracy', *Sociology*, vol. 1 (1967).

Hobsbawn, Eric J., 'The Labour Aristocracy in 19th c. Britain', in *Labouring Men: Studies in the History of Labour* (London, 1964).

Homans, G.C., *The Human Group* (London, 1950).

Indik, Bernard P., 'Some Effects of Organization Size on Member Attitudes and Behaviour', *Human Relations*, vol. 16 (1963).

— —, 'Relationship between Organization Size and Supervision Ratio', *Administrative Science Quarterly*, vol. 9 (1965).

— —, 'Organization Size and Member Participation: Some Empirical Tests of Alternative Explanations', *Human Relations*, vol. 18 (1965).

Ingham, Geoffrey K., 'Organizational Size, Orientation to Work and Industrial Behaviour', *Sociology*, vol. 1 (1967).

— —, 'Plant Size: Political Attitudes and Behaviour', *Sociological Review*, n.s. vol. 17 (1969).

Jasinski, Frank J., 'Technological Delimitation of Reciprocal Relationships', *Human Organization*, vol. 15 (1956).

Kadushin, Charles, 'Social Class and the Experience of Ill Health', in R. Bendix and S.M. Lipset, *Class, Status and Power* (2nd edn) (London, 1966), pp. 406-12.

Katz, Z., and Lazarsfeld, P.F., *Personal Influence* (Glencoe, Ill., 1954).

Kerchoff, A.G., 'Nuclear and Extended Family Relationships', in E. Shanas and F.G. Strieb (eds.), *Social Structure and the Family* (New Jersey, 1965).

Kerr, Clark, and Fisher, Lloyd H., 'Plant Sociology: The Elite and the Aborigines' in Mirra Komarovsky (ed.), *Common Frontiers of the Social Sciences* (Glencoe, Ill., 1954).

Kerr, W.A., 'Labour Turnover and its Correlates', *Journal of Applied Psychology*, vol. 31 (1949).

Klein, Josephine, *Samples from English Cultures*, vol. 1 (London, 1965).

Kornhauser, A., *Mental Health of the Industrial Worker* (New York, 1965).

Kyllonen, T.E., 'Social Characteristics of Active Trade Unionists', *American Journal of Sociology*, vol. 56 (1951).

Lipset, S.M., Trow, M.A. and Coleman, J.S., *Union Democracy* (Glencoe, Ill., 1956).

Lipset, S.M. and Bendix, R., *Social Mobility in Industrial Society* (London, 1959).

– –, *The First New Nation* (New York, 1963).

Lockwood, David, *The Blackcoated Worker* (London, 1958).

– –, 'The New Working Class', *European Journal of Sociology*, vol. 1 (1960).

– –, 'Sources of Variation in Working Class Images of Society', *Sociological Review*, vol. 14 (1966).

Long, J.R., *Labour Turnover under Full Employment* (Birmingham, 1951).

Lundquist, A., 'Absenteeism and Job Turnover as a Consequence of Unfavourable Job Adjustment', *Acta Sociologica*, vol. 3 (1958).

Marriott, R., 'Size of Working Group and Output', *Occupational Psychology*, vol. 23 (1949), 47-57.

Mayo, Elton, *The Social Problems of an Industrial Civilization* (London, 1949).

Merton, Robert, K., *Social Theory and Social Structure* (Glencoe, Ill., 1957).

Morse, Nancy, *Satisfaction in the White Collar Job* (Ann Arbor, 1953).

Palmer, Gladys, *The Reluctant Job Changer* (Philadelphia, 1962).

Parnes, H.S., *Research on Labour Mobility* (New York, 1954).

Parsons, Talcott, *The Social System* (London, 1951).

Poggi, G., 'A Main Theme of Contemporary Sociological Analysis: Its Achievements and Limitations', *British Journal of Sociology*, vol. 16 (1965).

Poidevin, S.L., 'A Study of Factors Affecting Labour Turnover', *Personnel Practice Bulletin*, vol. 1 (1949).

Revans, R.W., 'Industrial Morale and Size of Unit', *Political Quarterly*, vol. 27 (1956).

– –, 'Human Relations, Management and Size', in E.M. Hugh-Jones (ed.), *Human Relations and Modern Management* (Amsterdam, 1958), pp. 177-220.

Shepherd, R.D. and Walker, J., 'Absence from Work in Relation to Wage Level and Family Responsibilities', *British Journal of Industrial Medicine*, vol. 15 (1958).

Shimmin, Sylvia, 'Extra-Mural Factors Affecting Behaviour at Work', *Occupational Psychology*, vol. 36 (1962).

Silverman, David, 'Formal Organizations or Industrial Sociology: Towards a Social Action Analysis of Organizations', *Sociology*, vol. 2 (1968).

Simmel, Georg, 'The Number of Members as Determining the Form of the Group', *American Journal of Sociology*, vol. 8 (1902).

Smigel, E.O., 'Public Attitudes towards Stealing as related to the Size of the Victim Organization', *American Sociological Review*, vol. 21 (1956).

Stacey, Margaret, *Tradition and Change: A Study of Banbury* (London, 1960).

Stinchcombe, Arthur L., 'Bureaucratic and Craft Administration of Production: A Comparative Study', *Administrative Science Quarterly*, vol. 4 (1959).

Talacchi, S., 'Organizational Size, Individual Attitudes and Behaviour: An Empirical Study', *Administrative Science Quarterly*, vol. 5 (1960).
Terrien, F.W., and Mills, D.L., 'The Effect of Changing Size upon the Internal Structure of Organizations', *American Sociological Review*, vol. 20 (1955).
Thomas, E.J., 'Role Conceptions and Organization Size', *American Sociological Review*, vol. 24 (1959).
Touraine, Alain, and Ragazzi, O., *Ouvriers d'Origine Agricole* (Paris, 1961).
Tsouderous, John E., 'Organizational Change in Terms of a Series of Selected Variables', *American Sociological Review*, vol. 20 (1955).
Turner, Arthur N. and Lawrence, Paul R., *Industrial Jobs and the Worker* (Boston, 1965).
Turner, H.A., *Labour Relations in the Motor Industry* (London, 1967).

Walker, Charles, and Guest, Robert H., *Man on the Assembly Line* (Cambridge, Mass., 1955).
Weber, Max, *The Protestant Ethic and the Spirit of Capitalism* (London, 1930).
– –, *The Theory of Social and Economic Organization* (Glencoe, Ill., 1947).
Whyte, William Foote, *Money and Motivation* (New York, 1955).
– –, 'Human Relations – A Progress Report', in Amitai Etzioni (ed.), *Complex Organizations: A Sociological Reader* (New York, 1961).
Wilensky, H.L., 'Human Relations in the Workplace: An Appraisal of Some Recent Research', in C. Arensburg (ed.), *Research into Human Relations in Industry* (New York, 1957).
Wilensky, H.L. and Edwards, H., 'The Skidder: Ideological Adjustments of Downwardly Mobile Workers', *American Sociological Review*, vol. 24 (1959), 215-31.
Woodward, Joan, *Management and Technology* (London, 1958).
– –, *Industrial Organization: Theory and Practice* (London, 1965).
Wright Mills, C., *White Collar* (New York, 1957).

Zurcher, Louis A., Meadow, Arnold, and Zurcher, Susan Lee, 'Value Orientation, Role Conflict and Alienation from Work: A Cross Cultural Study', *American Sociological Review*, vol. 30 (1965), 539-48.
Zweig, Ferdinand, *The Worker in an Affluent Society* (London, 1961).

Index